mom's
SUGAR
SOLUTION

mom's SUGAR SOLUTION

150 Low-Sugar
Recipes for Your
Kids' Favorite Foods,
Sweet Treats, and More!

Laura Chalela Hoover,
MPH, RDN

Adams Media

New York London Toronto Sydney New Delhi

Adams Media
An Imprint of Simon & Schuster, Inc.
57 Littlefield Street
Avon, Massachusetts 02322

First Adams Media trade paperback edition JANUARY 2018

ADAMS MEDIA and colophon are trademarks of Simon and Schuster.

For information about special discounts for bulk purchases, please contact Simon & Schuster Special Sales at 1-866-506-1949 or business@simonandschuster.com.

The Simon & Schuster Speakers Bureau can bring authors to your live event. For more information or to book an event contact the Simon & Schuster Speakers Bureau at 1-866-248-3049 or visit our website at www.simonspeakers.com.

Interior design by Sylvia McArdle
Photographs by James Stefiuk
Food styled by Jen Solazzo
Images © Shutterstock

Manufactured in the United States of America

10 9 8 7 6 5 4 3 2 1

Library of Congress Cataloging-in-Publication Data has been applied for.

ISBN 978-1-5072-0485-6
ISBN 978-1-5072-0486-3 (ebook)

DEDICATION

A big hug of gratitude to Mike, Jack, Caitlin, Sarah, and Ricardo for always being my guinea pigs in the kitchen and my cheerleaders in all aspects of life.

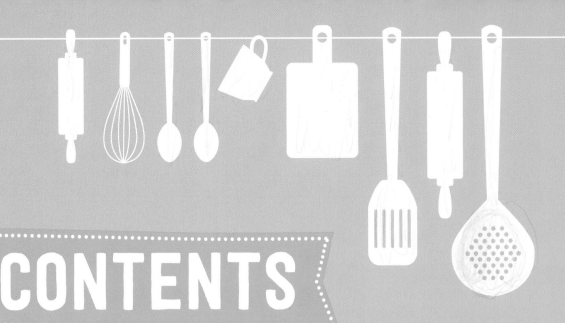

CONTENTS

CHAPTER 7: SIDES 135

CHAPTER 8: DESSERTS 161

CHAPTER 9:
DIPS, SAUCES, AND SPREADS . . 201

INTRODUCTION

Parenthood is full of unexpected challenges. One challenge that affects most of us: our children's obsession with sweets.

There's no doubt about it, feeding kids healthfully in today's world can be challenging. We live in a sugar-filled world: supersized candy at every checkout line, ice cream and Big Gulps at every sporting event, and cupcakes and sugar-filled goodie bags at birthday and holiday celebrations (which seem to come nearly every week). It can feel as if the world is conspiring against us.

If you feel like you're the only own who struggles with your child's sugar obsession, trust me, you're not. In a reader response survey I conducted on my website, *Smart Eating for Kids*, 30 percent said that their child's sugar obsession is their **number one food-related challenge**.

Truth be told, my own kids like sweets as much as the next kid. And, I like sweets a lot too. After all, we're human, and humans are wired to like sweets.

But it's not hopeless.

In this book, I share insights on why we crave sweets and offer several tried-and-true strategies to curb your family's cravings and respond to your child's relentless requests for the sweet stuff. I also provide guidance on sugar consumption so that you can set clear ground rules for your family. Once you've established the ground rules, it's about consistency and time.

Remember, when it comes to parenting kids, you're in it for the long haul. Change undeniably takes time. But small changes can add up and have a big impact. Have no doubt that the actions you take now will help guide your child toward a lifetime of healthier habits.

In addition to helpful strategies, this book contains 150 low-sugar recipes. My recipes are specifically designed for busy parents who don't necessarily love spending time in the kitchen, but who still value the importance of good food and healthy habits. Many of the recipes require just 10 minutes or less of hands-on time.

You'll notice that, collectively, the recipes emphasize a plant-based approach to eating. In other words, they feature a lot of fruits, vegetables, nuts, whole grains, and unsweetened dairy foods. This is not a vegan or vegetarian cookbook, by any means. However, fruits and vegetables, in particular, provide bundles of nutrients and antioxidants while also helping to satiate our sweet cravings.

In general, the desserts, snacks, and beverages in this book contain about 30–50 percent less sugar than you'll find in their traditional counterparts, but sometimes more and sometimes less. The recipes also feature natural sweeteners such as honey and maple syrup when possible, although traditional granulated cane sugar is used in many of the baked goods.

You'll see that each recipe includes basic nutrition facts, including the amount of added sugar. Think in terms of weekly proportions when choosing recipes. The sample meal plans in Appendix B provide inspiration on how you can balance out your family's sugar intake on any given day.

By implementing the strategies and following the recipes laid out in this book, it's my hope that your family will experience all the wonderful changes that can come from eating less sugar, from better moods and sleep to better heart health and body weight. So, let's get started on our low-sugar journey!

Chapter 1

THE LOW-SUGAR SOLUTION

You've seen the news stories and read the studies and you already know that sugar is not great for your kids. But what parent hasn't occasionally given in to the moaning or arguing over a sugary treat? As a society we've come to see sugar as a treat, a reward, and to cut that out can make you feel like you are denying yourself and your kids the "good stuff" in life.

While at times it may seem like you'll never be able to break your children's sugar habits, you should know that it is possible—and it is worth it. In this chapter, I'll give you the scoop on how much sugar is okay for your kids to eat in a day (because they still can eat some sugar!) and we'll look at some of the types of sugar and why some are worse for your children than others. We'll also talk about why your kids crave sugar and you'll learn how you can kick those cravings to the curb—realistically—without stressing out about how to get it done.

WHAT'S THE DEAL WITH SUGAR?

Today, it seems like sugar is everywhere you look and even the most careful shopper can still be fooled by food marketing and labels. You think you are buying a healthy, "natural" product, but that product may have more sugar than you've been led to believe. Not only is sugar in obvious foods, such as sugar-sweetened beverages and sweet treats, but food companies have also added it to a lot of unexpected foods, such as baby food, pasta sauces, and salad dressings. Sugars and syrups that are added to foods or beverages when they are processed or prepared are referred to as *added sugars*. Food manufacturers love putting added sugars—which are nothing more than empty calories—into processed foods because they are relatively cheap, they make food taste good, and those sugar cravings keep you coming back for more.

The large amount of products that are manufactured with added sugar can sometimes make you feel that you are fighting an uphill battle when you're trying to reduce sugar. But it is possible to avoid the hidden sugar traps when you do buy processed foods (as we all do!), and with the recipes in this book you can make reduced-sugar versions of some of those sweet treats your kids can't live without. Fortunately, you don't have to quit sugar cold turkey and stare white-knuckled at your cabinets. The strategies in this chapter will help you reduce your kids' sugar intake in ways that won't cause a family rebellion or make your kids feel like they're missing out on the yummy stuff.

When it comes to sugar in your diet, less is better. Most health authorities—including the 2015–2020 Dietary Guidelines for Americans and the American Heart Association—recommend that no more than 10 percent of our calories come from added sugars. This means no more than 25 grams (about 6 teaspoons) of added sugar for most children, no more than 37 grams (about 9 teaspoons) of added sugar for an adult who consumes 1,500 calories per day, and no more than 50 grams (about 12 teaspoons) of added sugar for an adult who consumes 2,000 calories per day. However, most people eat more added sugar than is recommended. On average, a person in the United States eats about 270 calories (68 grams) of added sugar a day. Children ages two to nineteen in the United States consume an average of about 310 calories (78 grams) of added sugar per day. That's nearly a half-cup of added sugar a day.

Natural Sugars

It's important to mention that when we talk about reducing sugars in our diets, we're talking about *added sugars*, not the sugars naturally found in whole foods such as fruit and milk. Fruit is loaded with beneficial nutrients and antioxidants that offer a number of health benefits, outweighing any concerns about the sugar they naturally contain. It's also difficult for most people to overeat foods that naturally contain sugar. In fact, nearly 80 percent of Americans fail to meet the recommendations for fruit consumption, so if anything, most of us need to eat more fruit. Likewise, unsweetened dairy foods, such as plain milk and plain yogurt, offer an assortment of beneficial nutrients, trivializing the natural sugar (lactose) they contain.

A Word about High-Fructose Corn Syrup

We've all heard of the infamous high-fructose corn syrup—in fact, it has become the topic of many debates about the food industry's practices. The fact is that food manufacturers use dozens of different types of sugar to add sweet flavors to packaged foods. While all added sugars should be limited, there is an especially strong argument for eliminating high-fructose corn syrup from your family's diet entirely. Not only is high-fructose corn syrup overused in our food supply (it's sweeter and cheaper than products made with cane sugar), but it is so quickly metabolized by the body that it's been shown to contribute to "fatty liver disease" and other metabolic issues.

The best ways to eliminate high-fructose corn syrup from your family's diet is to avoid sweetened, packaged foods in favor of whole foods and home-cooked meals and snacks. And when you do buy packaged foods, read the ingredients labels and avoid products that contain high-fructose corn syrup.

WHY DO KIDS CRAVE SUGAR?

Sugar cravings are not unusual; in fact, they are literally innate. Back in the caveman days when humans were mostly hunters and gatherers, it made sense to seek out something sweet. If you were a hunter, eating a sugary food gave you the quick burst of energy you needed to chase down your next meal. If you were foraging for foods, "sweet" generally signaled safe, while "bitter" signaled a potential poison. In other words, to increase your chances of survival, sweet foods were you friend.

A child's craving for sweets isn't meant to be a cruel joke on parents. It actually serves an important evolutionary purpose. Beyond helping a baby accept her mother's milk, a child's fondness for sweets also helps ensure that she will go on to accept other nutrient-dense foods, such as fruit.

However, kids don't just like sweet—they like *sweet*. In general, children prefer an intensity of sweetness that is almost twice the concentration of that which adults prefer. For example, while most adults would agree that a typical cola beverage tastes sweet, most kids would ideally prefer a sugar concentration that is twice as sweet as a cola. So, the next time your children eat or drink something sickly sweet—and you think they're from another planet for liking it—just remember that their taste buds are different from yours. What tastes sweet to you is just mildly sweet to them. The good news is that a child's strong preference for sweet flavors begins to decline during middle to late adolescence.

The fact is, the more sugar a child eats, the more a child craves. Research has shown that when children are repeatedly exposed to a sweetened beverage in a period of as little as 8 days, they give that beverage higher preference rankings and drink more of it at the end of the 8 days. This is a classic example of eat more sugar, crave more sugar.

THE LOW-SUGAR SOLUTION

First let's just say that to reduce your family's sugar intake you don't have to turn yourself into a "sugar cop" who monitors your child's every mouthful of food. That policy won't work for you or your child and will most likely just lead to more unneeded stress when your child sneaks treats in rebellion. The recipes in this book, along with the following twelve strategies, are designed to help you decrease your family's sugar intake in a balanced, practical, and family-friendly way. These recipes feature fruits, vegetables, nuts, whole grains, and unsweetened dairy foods that will fill your family's bellies so that their nutrient needs are being met, which in turn will help cut back on sugar cravings.

You'll find there are many benefits to a low-sugar diet including improvement in everyone's sleep habits. Eating sugar triggers the release of the hormone cortisol, which can interfere with sleep. Once you and your family cut back on sugar, everyone should be more alert during the day and get a more restful sleep at night.

While the goal is to eat as little sugar as possible, the reality is, we still live in a sugar-laden world. Sweet treats are a part of our culture and our celebrations. There are times you'll want to indulge and that's okay. In these cases, portion size is key, as is balancing out the rest of your choices throughout the day. In Appendix B you'll find several sample meal plans that show what you can make and serve on any given day. Each of the days includes a sweet treat and still comes in under 25 grams of added sugar, which is the recommended limit for most kids. There's no need to deprive your family of celebratory sweets, but you can and should be smart about it.

Following are some simple strategies that can help you reduce your family's overall sugar intake.

1. Find Balance

When it comes to monitoring your children's sugar intake, there is a fine line between being overly restrictive and overly indulgent. When parents are too restrictive with sugar, their kids often become obsessed with the "forbidden fruit" and tend to binge on sugar. When parents are too indulgent, their kids never learn smart eating habits.

Find balance between overpolicing and spoiling by being firm but not rigid. Be clear on your family's sugar rules, but be willing to make exceptions based on your good judgment. Use reasoning and structure to encourage your child to make healthy eating choices, while still respecting your child's preferences. Remember, the ultimate goal is to empower your child to make healthy choices, even when you're not supervising. The more you act as a "sugar consultant" versus a "sugar cop," the better your child will learn to control his or her own sugar intake.

2. Make Small Changes

As you transition to a low-sugar diet, gradually decrease the sugar in your family's diet over time rather than making a drastic cut all at once. Your family will be less likely to notice the change and, with time, will begin to appreciate the natural sweetness of whole foods rather than the shockingly strong sweet taste of added sugars.

Small changes can be made in all sorts of different ways throughout the day or week. For example, opt for natural peanut butter with no sugar added, replace a daily sugary treat with a piece of fresh fruit, or mix together your child's regular high-sugar cereal with a low-sugar cereal until you can eventually wean the high-sugar cereal out of rotation.

3. Break the Sweet Cycle

In our culture nearly every emotion is rewarded with a sugary treat, creating a cycle of sweet-dependence. Develop a list of when you most often give your child sweets and brainstorm some alternatives.

For example, if your child is upset, work on deep-breathing exercises instead of giving him candy. If he's bored, challenge him to a round of jumping jacks. If he's done a good job at something, put a token in a reward jar. Teaching your child how to manage emotions in ways that don't involve food is a skill that will benefit him for life.

While it's normal to be cranky for a week or two while you ditch sweets, once you are past the hump, you'll no longer have to deal with the dreaded sugar crash, which translates to more stable moods, less irritability, and fewer tantrums—for you and your children.

4. Set Clear Ground Rules

Decide how many sweets your children can eat in a day or week, then consistently stick with it. In general, one small treat a day is a good rule. Once they've eaten their treat, they're done for the day. If they ask for a second treat during the day, simply remind them that they've already had their treat for the day and offer to put whatever's tempting them "on hold" for tomorrow.

5. Be a Good Role Model

As a parent you know that it's important to practice what you preach. And your own sugar habits are no exception. Research shows that moms who routinely add sugar to their own foods have kids who are significantly more likely to prefer drinks and food with added sugar as compared to children whose mothers report never adding sugar to foods at home. Do your best to make your low-sugar lifestyle something the whole family adopts, beginning with yourself.

6. Keep Sweets Out of the Home

While there are a plethora of tempting treats at every turn, a significant portion of the added sugar we eat is eaten at home. A simple way to cut back on added sugar is to keep it out of your house.

Plus, it's easier to say no one time by refusing to buy candy or sweets at the grocery store than it is to have treats in the house and needing to say no repeatedly throughout the day. Make your life as easy as possible.

7. Stay Sugar Neutral

It's tempting to talk about how treats are "bad" for you. However, this can send mixed messages to kids, especially young ones. While your intention is simply to describe a food's nutritional attributes (or lack thereof), young children may internalize the description and hear, "If that food is bad and I like it, that must mean I'm bad too."

Instead, stay neutral and focus on your ground rules. Sweets and treats aren't good or bad; they are simply foods that should be enjoyed once in a while (e.g., once a day or three times a week) and in small portions.

8. Prioritize the Good Stuff

When you fill up on wholesome, nourishing foods, you naturally crowd out the junk. At each meal and snack, ask yourself, "Is there another fruit, vegetable, or whole grain that I could easily add?" The more you get into the habit of filling up on healthy stuff, the less room there is in your belly for the sugary stuff.

9. Snack Wisely

Snacks shouldn't be random handouts. A snack should have a planned time and place and represent food that you control. When putting together a snack, remember that the best snack options are always fresh, real, unprocessed foods. Aim to include at least two of the following food groups with each snack: fruits, vegetables, whole grains, protein, nuts/seeds, or dairy foods. For example, an apple with peanut butter, peaches with yogurt, carrots with hummus, or a half of a sandwich made on whole-grain bread and stuffed with veggies all make for simple, nourishing, flavorful snacks.

Once your family adjusts to eating less processed snacks, you'll be surprised at just how often your kids will crave these fresh, whole foods.

10. Keep Hunger at Bay

When your body needs a boost of energy, sugar is the quickest way to get it—which often leads to sugar cravings. Eating small amounts of food on a regular schedule can help satiate your child before the sugar cravings strike. Young kids need to eat about every two hours. Older kids and adults can space out meals and snacks to about every three or four hours. Foods that contain protein, fiber, and/or healthy fats can help keep you satiated longer.

11. Emphasize Naturally Sweet Foods

Earlier in this chapter we talked about how humans evolved to prefer sweet foods as a way to ensure kids would accept naturally sweet and nourishing foods, such as fruit. As you and your family cut back on sugary processed foods, embrace evolution by replacing the fake stuff with the sweets that nature intended: apples, pears, bananas, peaches, plums, grapes, dates, figs, melons, berries, and more.

12. Start Now

The longer a habit is in place, the harder it is to break. While your child may resist the meaningful changes you're attempting to make now, know that his or her life will be so much better and healthier because of it. There is no time like the present to make your family's health a priority, so let's get cooking!

Chapter 2

BREAKFAST

It's no surprise that a good breakfast can set the tone for a successful day. Kids who eat a healthy breakfast tend to have more energy, behave better, perform better in school, eat healthier throughout the day, and have better overall nutrient intake. These are qualities you undoubtedly want for your children.

Yet, in many homes, breakfast is often nothing more than disguised dessert. Case in point: some kid-favorite cereals can contain as much as 15 grams of sugar per serving while many pastries are loaded with 30 grams or more of sugar. Yikes!

The recipes in this chapter will help you start your family's day with wholesome goodness. They collectively feature an assortment of whole grains, nuts, seeds, and fruit to power your child's brain and body the natural way. Whether you're looking for grab-and-go breakfasts, make-ahead breakfasts, or leisurely breakfasts for lazy mornings, these recipes offer a variety of ways to start the day off right.

PEACHY CREAM PANCAKES

Fresh peaches are always one of the highlights of summer. When picking peaches from your farmers' market or grocery store, be sure to smell them and give them a little squeeze. A perfectly ripe peach should smell the way you want it to taste, as well as give a little bit under the pressure of your fingertips. This recipe pairs sweet, juicy peaches with honeyed whole grains for a sunny start to your morning.

1 large egg

1 cup sour cream

¼ teaspoon pure vanilla extract

2 tablespoons honey

¼ teaspoon salt

¼ teaspoon ground cinnamon

½ cup white whole-wheat flour

¼ cup all-purpose flour

1 teaspoon baking powder

½ teaspoon baking soda

2 teaspoons unsalted butter, divided

1 cup peeled, diced peaches

1 cup peeled, sliced peaches (for garnish)

½ cup fresh raspberries (for garnish)

1. Heat a large griddle or skillet on medium-low heat.

2. Whisk together egg, sour cream, vanilla, and honey in a large bowl.

3. In a medium bowl, mix together salt, cinnamon, flours, baking powder, and baking soda.

4. Fold flour mixture into egg mixture, mixing until just a few small lumps remain, about 1 minute.

5. Melt 1 teaspoon butter in the griddle or skillet, then ladle in ¼ cup batter per pancake to make 4 pancakes. Sprinkle ⅛ cup diced peaches over the batter of each pancake.

6. Flip pancakes when they are dry around the edges and bubbling on top, about 3 minutes.

7. Cook until pancakes are golden brown on the underside, about 2 minutes.

8. Add remaining teaspoon butter to griddle. Repeat process with remaining batter and diced peaches. Garnish with fresh raspberries and sliced peaches and serve warm.

Calories: 300 | Fat: 13g | Protein: 7g | Sodium: 410mg | Fiber: 4g | Carbohydrates: 34g | Sugar: 18g | Added Sugar: 9g

The Super Fruit of Summer

Peaches are a sweet super fruit, packing in more than twenty different nutrients, notably beta-carotene, an antioxidant needed for good vision, a strong immune system, and healthy skin. When fresh peaches aren't in season, opt for frozen or canned that are packed in water with no sugar added.

2 large eggs

½ cup skim milk

1 teaspoon pure vanilla extract

2 tablespoons cream cheese

4 slices sprouted whole-grain
bread

½ cup frozen wild blueberries,
slightly defrosted (10 minutes)

Cooking spray

WILD BLUEBERRY-STUFFED FRENCH TOAST

Wild blueberries are drastically different from the conventional blueberries you typically find in the produce section of your local supermarket. Not only are they smaller in size, but they are bursting with a more intense, sweet, and tangy taste compared to cultivated blueberries. They hold their shape, color, and texture well, making them a great option for baked goods. Luckily, you can find wild blueberries in the freezer section of most major supermarkets, allowing you to make this flavorful French toast any time of the year, even when wild blueberries aren't in season.

1. In a small bowl, whisk together eggs, milk, and vanilla until thoroughly combined, about 2 minutes. Set aside.

2. Spread cream cheese on 2 bread slices and top with blueberries. It's okay if the blueberries are still a little frozen; they will warm up when you grill the French toast. Top with remaining bread slices and use a fork to press around the edges to seal.

3. Spray a large skillet with nonstick cooking spray and heat over medium heat until skillet is hot.

4. Dip sandwiches in egg mixture for a few seconds on each side; let excess egg mixture drip off.

5. Cook sandwiches 2–3 minutes on each side until golden brown. Slice and serve.

Calories: 330 | Fat: 11g | Protein: 17g | Sodium: 140mg | Fiber: 2g | Carbohydrates: 40g | Sugar: 6g | Added Sugar: 0g

STRAWBERRY-STUDDED BELGIAN WAFFLES

Serves 4
(serving size: 1 waffle)

PREP: 20 minutes
COOK: 10 minutes

Fresh-picked, fragrant strawberries have a vibrant, natural sweetness that can boost the flavor of any dish. In this recipe, you'll mix diced strawberries right into the waffle batter so you get that burst of sweetness in every bite. You may want to make a double batch and freeze any remaining waffles for a grab-and-go breakfast another day. For an extra nutrient boost, try smearing these waffles with homemade creamy peanut butter instead of more traditional sugary toppings.

½ cup whole-wheat flour

½ cup all-purpose flour

Zest of 1 medium lemon

2 teaspoons baking powder

¼ teaspoon salt

1 large egg

1 cup skim milk

1 teaspoon pure vanilla extract

¼ cup coconut oil, melted

½ cup hulled and diced fresh strawberries

3 tablespoons water

1 tablespoon pure maple syrup

1 tablespoon fresh lemon juice

Cooking spray

1. Preheat waffle iron.

2. In a medium bowl, mix together flours, lemon zest, baking powder, and salt.

3. In a large bowl, whisk together egg, milk, and vanilla until thoroughly combined, about 1 minute. Add flour mixture to egg mixture and mix until just combined, about 30 seconds. Stir in coconut oil until mixture is smooth, about 1 minute.

4. In a small saucepan, stir together strawberries, water, syrup, and lemon juice over medium heat. Heat the mixture about 3 minutes until it begins to bubble slightly, then lower heat and simmer 5 minutes, stirring gently.

5. Swirl strawberry mixture into batter. Spray waffle iron with cooking spray. Ladle batter into waffle iron and cook until waffles are golden and crispy, about 2 minutes. Serve warm.

Calories: 290 | Fat: 15g | Protein: 7g | Sodium: 200mg | Fiber: 2g | Carbohydrates: 32g | Sugar: 7g | Added Sugar: 3g

WHOLE-GRAIN PUMPKIN WAFFLES

Pumpkin purée is an easy, nutrient-rich ingredient to work with that lends big flavor to baked goods. This recipe pairs it with whole grains and a simplified version of traditional pumpkin pie spices, resulting in all the flavor of pumpkin pie without any of the guilt. Put on your fuzzy slippers and enjoy these pumpkin waffles with a cup of warm Almond Milk Chai Latte (see Chapter 3) for a cozy, satisfying start to the day.

1 cup whole-wheat pastry flour

½ cup all-purpose flour

2 teaspoons ground cinnamon

½ teaspoon ground nutmeg

½ teaspoon ground ginger

¼ teaspoon baking soda

2 teaspoons baking powder

½ teaspoon salt

2 large eggs, beaten

1½ cups skim milk

3 tablespoons unsalted butter, melted

2 tablespoons pure maple syrup

½ cup pumpkin purée

Cooking spray

1. Preheat waffle iron.

2. In a medium bowl, whisk together flours, cinnamon, nutmeg, ginger, baking soda, baking powder, and salt.

3. In a large bowl, whisk together eggs, milk, butter, and syrup.

4. Add flour mixture to egg mixture and mix until just combined, about 30 seconds.

5. Gently fold in the pumpkin purée, stirring until combined but not overmixed, about 1 minute.

6. Spray waffle iron with cooking spray. Ladle batter into waffle iron and cook until waffles are golden and crispy, about 5 minutes. Repeat with remaining batter. Serve warm.

Calories: 240 | Fat: 3.5g | Protein: 11g | Sodium: 160mg | Fiber: 1g | Carbohydrates: 45g | Sugar: 12g | Added Sugar: 6g

SOUR CREAM COFFEE CAKE

Serves 12

PREP: 20 minutes
COOK: 60 minutes

Coffee cake is the perfect breakfast to have on hand when you have out-of-town visitors staying with you. Inevitably, everyone is ready for breakfast at different times. This coffee cake, served with a vibrant fruit platter, is a low-maintenance solution that makes everyone happy as they roll in and out of your kitchen, each on his or her own time zone.

Cooking spray

2 tablespoons unsalted butter

¼ cup granulated sugar

¼ cup honey

1⅓ cups unsweetened applesauce

2 large eggs

2 teaspoons pure vanilla extract

2 cups all-purpose flour

1 teaspoon baking powder

¾ teaspoon baking soda

½ teaspoon salt

¾ cup sour cream

½ cup chopped pecans

1. Preheat oven to 350°F. Grease a 9" Bundt pan with cooking spray and set aside.

2. In a mixer, cream together butter, sugar, and honey until fluffy, about 2 minutes. Add applesauce and mix, scraping down sides of bowl to make sure everything is incorporated, about 1 more minute.

3. Add eggs and vanilla to mixer (1 egg at a time) and scrape down bowl, incorporating all ingredients.

4. Add flour, baking powder, baking soda, and salt. Mix until dough comes together, about 2 minutes, but don't overmix or the flour will get tough.

5. Add sour cream to batter and mix until smooth, about 1 minute.

6. Fold in pecans.

7. Spoon batter into Bundt pan and bake 50–60 minutes, until lightly golden and a toothpick inserted into the center comes out clean.

8. Allow cake to cool in the pan completely, then flip onto a large tray. Wrap well and store in the refrigerator up to 1 week.

Calories: 210 | Fat: 8g | Protein: 4g | Sodium: 210mg | Fiber: 1g | Carbohydrates: 31g | Sugar: 13g | Added Sugar: 10g

⅔ cup coconut oil, melted

⅓ cup honey

4 large eggs

2 teaspoons pure vanilla extract

3 ripe medium bananas

3¼ cups whole-wheat flour

2 teaspoons baking soda

1 teaspoon salt

½ teaspoon ground cinnamon

½ cup hot water

½ cup chopped walnuts

BANANA WALNUT MINI MUFFINS

These three-bite mini muffins are perfectly moist and delicious, flavored with a perfect combination of bananas, honey, and cinnamon. Try them for breakfast with a Cinnamon Smoothie (see recipe in this chapter). Or have them as a snack, smeared with creamy homemade peanut butter. Hint: make a double batch and freeze in an airtight container for an emergency stash of morning goodness.

1. Preheat oven to 350°F. Line a 24-cup mini muffin pan with paper liners.

2. In a large bowl, beat together coconut oil and honey using a hand mixer on medium speed, about 30 seconds. Scrape down sides of bowl and beat again for another 30 seconds. Add eggs, vanilla, and bananas; mix on low speed, about 1 minute, scraping down sides of bowl to incorporate all ingredients.

3. In a separate large bowl, use a fork to mix together flour, baking soda, salt, and cinnamon. Add hot water, stirring with fork until well combined, about 2 minutes.

4. Slowly pour flour mixture into bowl with banana mixture, mixing on medium speed, about 1 minute. Turn off mixer, add walnuts, and use fork to evenly disperse walnuts throughout batter.

5. Use a small ice cream scoop or a tablespoon to scoop the batter into the prepared mini muffin pan. The batter should fill about ¾ of each cup.

6. Bake 10–15 minutes or until a toothpick inserted in the center of a muffin comes out clean. Cool in muffin pan, then store in a tightly wrapped container up to 1 week or freeze.

Calories: 170 | Fat: 9g | Protein: 4g | Sodium: 210mg | Fiber: 2g | Carbohydrates: 19g | Sugar: 6g | Added Sugar: 4g

CARROT MINI MUFFINS

Loaded with carrots and sweetened naturally with applesauce and honey, these bite-sized muffins are a good nut-free option for a school snack or lunch. If food allergies aren't an issue, add ½ cup chopped walnuts when you add the carrots to the batter. Or if you want an extra burst of sweetness, add ½ cup raisins.

1. Preheat oven to 350°F. Line a 24-cup mini muffin pan with paper or foil liners.

2. In a mixer, mix together butter, honey, egg, and vanilla until fully combined, about 1 minute.

3. Turn mixer off and add flour, baking soda, cinnamon, nutmeg, and salt. Turn mixer on and mix about 2 minutes. The batter will look thick, but that's okay.

4. Slowly add applesauce and carrots to batter; mix about 1 minute. The batter will start to look a little runnier now and more like a muffin batter.

5. Use a small ice cream scoop or a tablespoon to scoop batter into the prepared mini muffin pan. The batter should fill about ¾ of each cup.

6. Bake 10–15 minutes or until a toothpick inserted in the center of a muffin comes out clean.

7. Cool in muffin pan, then store in a tightly wrapped container up to 1 week or freeze.

Calories: 80 | Fat: 4g | Protein: 1g | Sodium: 160mg | Fiber: 1g | Carbohydrates: 11g | Sugar: 5g | Added Sugar: 4g

Serves 24
(serving size: 1 muffin)

PREP: 15 minutes
COOK: 15 minutes

½ cup unsalted butter, melted

⅓ cup honey

1 large egg

2 teaspoons pure vanilla extract

1½ cups whole-wheat flour

1 teaspoon baking soda

1½ teaspoons ground cinnamon

½ teaspoon ground nutmeg

1 teaspoon salt

1 cup unsweetened applesauce

1 cup peeled and grated carrots

2 tablespoons unsalted butter, softened

½ cup honey

½ cup unsweetened applesauce

1 large egg

½ cup plain low-fat yogurt

1 teaspoon pure vanilla extract

1½ cups all-purpose flour

1½ teaspoons baking powder

1 teaspoon baking soda

½ teaspoon salt

⅛ cup chia seeds

¾ cup fresh raspberries

The Power of Chia

Chia seeds are edible seeds that have very high antioxidant activity, making them a great food to incorporate into your family's diet. In addition to adding them to muffins or other baked goods, try sprinkling them on cereal and yogurt or adding them to smoothies, vegetables, or rice.

RASPBERRY CHIA MINI MUFFINS

Sweet, fresh raspberries and golden honey meld together to make these mouthwatering mini muffins. The addition of chia seeds gives them an extra boost of protein and omega-3s. For a more complete meal, crumble a mini muffin and sprinkle it on top of Greek yogurt, along with more fresh raspberries, to make a satisfying yogurt parfait.

1. Preheat oven to 350°F. Line a 24-cup mini muffin pan with paper or foil liners.

2. In a mixer, mix together butter, honey, and applesauce on medium-low speed until butter is well dispersed, about 2 minutes.

3. Add egg and mix on medium-low speed until incorporated, about 1 minute, using a spatula to scrape down sides of bowl as needed to make sure butter is incorporated.

4. Add yogurt and vanilla; mix to combine on medium-low speed for 1 additional minute.

5. Add flour, baking powder, baking soda, and salt and mix on low speed until a batter forms, about 2 minutes.

6. Remove bowl from mixer and stir in chia seeds by hand. Then gently fold in raspberries. You don't want to fold them in too much, as your dough will turn pink if overhandled; 1–2 quick turns with a spatula will be enough.

7. Use a small ice cream scoop or a tablespoon to scoop batter into the mini muffin pan. The batter should fill about ¾ of each cup.

8. Bake 10–15 minutes or until a toothpick inserted in the center of a muffin comes out clean.

9. Cool in pan, then store in a tightly wrapped container up to 1 week or freeze.

Calories: 70 | Fat: 1.5g | Protein: 2g | Sodium: 110mg | Fiber: 1g | Carbohydrates: 14g | Sugar: 6g | Added Sugar: 5g

BANANA WALNUT BAKED OATMEAL

This warm, comforting oatmeal is good for the body and brain. It pairs together walnuts and ground flaxseed, which are both good sources of omega-3 fatty acids. Plus, each serving packs in 20 percent of the recommended amount of daily fiber. Be sure to use rolled oats, not instant oats, to get the hearty texture that makes oatmeal so satisfying.

Cooking spray

2 cups rolled oats

½ cup chopped walnuts, divided

1 teaspoon baking powder

1½ teaspoons ground cinnamon

½ teaspoon salt

3 tablespoons pure maple syrup

2 cups skim milk

1 large egg

2 tablespoons unsalted butter, melted

2 teaspoons pure vanilla extract

2 tablespoons ground flaxseed

2 ripe medium bananas, cut into ½" pieces

1. Preheat oven to 375°F. Grease an 8" square baking dish with cooking spray.

2. In a large bowl, mix together oats, ¼ cup walnuts, baking powder, cinnamon, and salt until well-mixed, about 30 seconds.

3. In a separate large bowl, whisk together syrup, milk, egg, butter, vanilla, and flaxseed, about 1 minute.

4. Place bananas in a single layer in the prepared baking dish, then evenly sprinkle in oat mixture.

5. Slowly and evenly drizzle milk mixture on top of oats. If any milk is pooling on top of oats, use a wooden spoon to gently tap it down through the oats, without disturbing the banana layer.

6. Sprinkle remaining walnuts on top.

7. Bake 35–45 minutes until mostly firm with just a little jiggle in the center. Remove from oven and let cool a few minutes before serving.

Calories: 320 | Fat: 14g | Protein: 10g | Sodium: 250mg | Fiber: 5g | Carbohydrates: 41g | Sugar: 16g | Added Sugar: 6g

Breakfast with Benefits

Oatmeal is one of the best ways to start the day. Research has shown that kids who eat oatmeal tend to have better nutrient intake, better overall diet quality, and less likelihood of being overweight or obese.

SUGAR COOKIE OATMEAL

Mix up your regular oatmeal routine with this recipe, which incorporates quinoa flakes, a source of complete protein. Quinoa flakes are simply quinoa that has been rolled into a very thin flake. Don't be deceived by the warm sugar cookie flavor of this oatmeal; each serving has just ½ teaspoon honey.

1. In a medium saucepan over medium-high heat, combine oats, quinoa, salt, cinnamon, honey, and coconut milk. Bring to a boil, then reduce to a simmer. Cook until liquid is absorbed, about 3–5 minutes.

2. Remove from heat and stir in vanilla. Serve warm.

½ cup rolled oats

½ cup quinoa flakes

⅛ teaspoon salt

¼ teaspoon ground cinnamon

2 teaspoons honey

2½ cups unsweetened coconut milk

1 teaspoon pure vanilla extract

Calories: 250 | Fat: 9g | Protein: 6g | Sodium: 150mg | Fiber: 2g | Carbohydrates: 37g | Sugar: 5g | Added Sugar: 3g

RASPBERRY ALMOND OVERNIGHT OATS

3 cups unsweetened almond milk

1 tablespoon honey

1 teaspoon pure vanilla extract

½ teaspoon pure almond extract

2½ cups rolled oats

1 cup fresh raspberries, divided

4 ounces sliced almonds

If you've never tried overnight oats, get ready for your morning routine to become insanely simpler. The night before, you simply assemble all the ingredients into mason jars, refrigerate, and let the magic of time do the work for you. When you wake up, voilà! Breakfast is waiting. You can increase or decrease this recipe depending on how many people you plan to serve each morning. I generally make enough to last about 3 days.

1. In a medium bowl, stir together almond milk, honey, vanilla, and almond extract. Stir in oats.

2. In a small bowl, mash half the raspberries with the back of a fork.

3. Fill 6 small mason jars halfway with oat mixture.

4. Divide mashed raspberries between mason jars to create a thin layer. Top with remaining oat mixture.

5. Garnish each with remaining whole raspberries and a sprinkle of almonds.

6. Refrigerate overnight. In the morning, serve cold or zap in the microwave until just warmed, about 1 minute.

Calories: 280 | Fat: 14g | Protein: 9g | Sodium: 95mg | Fiber: 7g | Carbohydrates: 33g | Sugar: 5g | Added Sugar: 3g

MANGO COCONUT YOGURT PARFAIT

Serves 2

PREP: **5 minutes**
COOK: **N/A**

Yogurt parfaits are a great way to layer together multiple food groups for a nutrient-rich breakfast. This tropical-inspired recipe uses coconut yogurt for a dairy-free alternative, but feel free to use plain Greek yogurt. Yogurt parfaits are also a great way to teach kids basic skills in the kitchen. Even kids as young as three or four years old can be in charge of layering the ingredients.

2 cups unsweetened coconut milk yogurt, divided

4 tablespoons slivered almonds, divided

4 tablespoons unsweetened shredded coconut, divided

½ teaspoon ground cinnamon, divided

1 cup diced fresh mango, divided

1. Scoop ½ cup yogurt into a small mason jar. Repeat with a second mason jar.

2. Top each with 1 tablespoon almonds, 1 tablespoon shredded coconut, ⅛ teaspoon cinnamon, and ¼ cup mango.

3. Top each with remaining yogurt and toppings in the same order, divided evenly. Enjoy or refrigerate up to 2 days.

Calories: 360 | Fat: 23g | Protein: 4g | Sodium: 15mg | Fiber: 5g | Carbohydrates: 42g | Sugar: 28g |
Added Sugar: 0g

BLUEBERRY ALMOND GRANOLA

Serves 12
(serving size: ½ cup)

PREP: 5 minutes
COOK: 25 minutes

Most granolas are loaded with sugar. This granola gets its sweetness naturally, from pure maple syrup, and has about half the sugar of regular granola. Using freeze-dried blueberries makes this a kid favorite and cuts down on the prep time for you. Win-win! Make sure you use raw almonds, as you'll be cooking them along with the granola. If you already have roasted almonds on hand, they are perfectly fine to use, just add them after you take the granola out of the oven so the almonds don't burn.

3 cups rolled oats

1½ cups raw slivered almonds

1½ teaspoons kosher salt

½ teaspoon ground cinnamon

½ cup olive oil

½ cup pure maple syrup

1 teaspoon pure vanilla extract

1 cup freeze-dried blueberries

1. Preheat oven to 350°F. Line a rimmed baking sheet with parchment paper.

2. Mix together oats, almonds, salt, and cinnamon in a large bowl. Pour in the oil, syrup, and vanilla; stir until thoroughly combined, about 1 minute.

3. Scoop granola onto baking sheet and bake 25 minutes or until mixture is golden, stirring halfway through the baking time. Keep in mind that the granola will continue to cook slightly after you take it out of the oven, so don't worry if it seems a little wet.

4. Remove from oven and stir in freeze-dried blueberries.

5. Let cool before enjoying or storing in an airtight container up to 2 weeks. For longer shelf life, store in the refrigerator.

Calories: 280 | Fat: 17g | Protein: 5g | Sodium: 290mg | Fiber: 4g | Carbohydrates: 28g | Sugar: 11g | Added Sugar: 8g

PREP: 5 minutes
COOK: 25 minutes

CRANBERRY WALNUT GRANOLA

One of the best things about granola is that you can customize the ingredients to make everyone's taste buds happy. While we all have our favorite flavors and foods, taste preferences naturally change with the seasons. When autumn rolls in, this cranberry-walnut combo is a crowd-pleaser. In addition to having it for breakfast, you can nosh on this satisfying granola as a snack or use it as a healthier ice-cream topping.

3 cups rolled oats

1 cup raw chopped walnuts

1½ teaspoons kosher salt

½ teaspoon ground cinnamon

½ teaspoon ground cardamom

½ cup olive oil

½ cup honey

1 teaspoon pure vanilla extract

½ cup lightly sweetened dried cranberries

1. Preheat oven to 350°F. Line a rimmed baking sheet with p archment paper.

2. Mix together oats, walnuts, salt, cinnamon, and cardamom in a large bowl. Pour in oil, honey, and vanilla; stir until thoroughly combined, about 1 minute.

3. Turn granola onto baking sheet and bake 25 minutes or until mixture is golden, stirring halfway through baking time. Keep in mind that the granola will continue to cook slightly after you take it out of the oven, so don't worry if it seems a little wet.

4. Remove from oven and stir in cranberries.

5. Let cool before enjoying or storing in an airtight container up to 2 weeks. For longer shelf life, store in the refrigerator.

Benefits of Cranberries

Research shows that tart cranberries reduce inflammation in the body and help keep the urinary tract healthy. Cranberries are usually sweetened because they are lower in natural sugars than most berries, which is why they taste so tart. Choose lightly sweetened dried cranberries to keep added sugars in check.

Calories: 280 | Fat: 17g | Protein: 4g | Sodium: 290mg | Fiber: 3g | Carbohydrates: 31g | Sugar: 11g | Added Sugar: 8g

GREEN MONSTER SMOOTHIE

There's something about starting your day with a green smoothie that helps set your taste buds and attitude for a successful day. The secret to this smoothie is that the apple and lemon give it a refreshing twist, while also helping to mask the bitter taste of the greens. To speed along morning prep time, prepare and measure out all the ingredients the night before, then store in a mason jar in the refrigerator. In the morning, simply blend and enjoy.

1 medium banana, sliced

1 medium green apple, cored and chopped

½ cup sliced cucumber (unpeeled)

2 cups baby spinach

Juice of 1 medium lemon

Use a blender to purée all ingredients until smooth, about 1 minute. Enjoy immediately.

Calories: 120 | Fat: 0g | Protein: 3g | Sodium: 45mg | Fiber: 5g | Carbohydrates: 31g | Sugar: 18g | Added Sugar: 0g

1 cup frozen mango chunks

1 cup frozen pineapple chunks

½ cup frozen sliced banana

1½ cups coconut water

1 teaspoon honey

1 tablespoon pomegranate seeds

1 tablespoon unsweetened shredded coconut

2 lime wedges

TROPICAL SMOOTHIE

This refreshing smoothie will make you feel like you're relaxing on a beach in the tropics. Using frozen fruit is not only the ultimate shortcut, but also delivers extra nutritional appeal. Fruit normally begins to lose nutrients the minute it's harvested, and that nutrient loss continues to happen while fruits are transported to supermarket shelves. Because most frozen fruits are frozen shortly after they're harvested, their nutrients are "locked in," offering better nutrient content and flavor.

1. Use a blender to purée mango, pineapple, banana, coconut water, and honey on high speed until smooth, about 2 minutes.

2. Pour into 2 serving glasses. Sprinkle pomegranate seeds and coconut on top, dividing equally. Garnish the rim of each glass with a lime wedge. Enjoy immediately.

Calories: 190 | Fat: 2g | Protein: 2g | Sodium: 10mg | Fiber: 4g | Carbohydrates: 43g | Sugar: 22g | Added Sugar: 3g

¼ cup rolled oats, ground into a powder

1 cup unsweetened almond milk

½ cup plain low-fat Greek yogurt

1 medium banana, sliced and frozen (if using fresh, add ¼ cup ice cubes)

1 teaspoon honey

1 teaspoon ground cinnamon

CINNAMON SMOOTHIE

Adding oatmeal to smoothies is a great way to sneak in a bit of extra fiber. The trick is to grind the oats into a powder before adding it to the smoothie. You can do this in a high-powdered blender, coffee grinder, or food processor. The result is a thicker smoothie that holds its substance longer, making this an especially good technique to use for smoothies for any slow sippers in your home.

Combine all ingredients in a blender and blend until smooth, about 1 minute. Enjoy immediately.

Calories: 210 | Fat: 5g | Protein: 15g | Sodium: 135mg | Fiber: 3g | Carbohydrates: 30g | Sugar: 15g | Added Sugar: 3g

BLUEBERRY SCONES

Serves 12
(serving size: 1 scone)

PREP: 20 minutes
COOK: 30 minutes

These soft, slightly sweet scones are flavored with fresh blueberries and orange zest. Unlike most highly processed scones, they are made with 100% whole-wheat flour, resulting in an earthier, more filling breakfast treat. For a satisfying breakfast or snack, enjoy your scone with a cup of tea and a small bowl of plain Greek yogurt.

2 cups plus 1 tablespoon whole-wheat flour, divided

2¼ teaspoons baking powder

1½ tablespoons granulated sugar

½ teaspoon salt

¼ cup cold, unsalted butter

2 large eggs

⅓ cup heavy cream

2 teaspoons fresh-grated orange zest

1 cup fresh blueberries

1. Preheat oven to 350°F.

2. In a large mixing bowl, sift together 2 cups flour, baking powder, sugar, and salt.

3. Use two knives or your hands to cut butter into the flour mixture until it's the size of small peas, about 1 minute. Do not overmix. Set aside.

4. In a medium mixing bowl, beat the eggs. Add heavy cream and beat with an electric hand mixer on medium until well combined, about 1 minute.

5. Make a well in the dry ingredients. Pour egg mixture into the center. Add orange zest. Gently mix on low just until the dry ingredients are moistened; do not overmix. Gently fold in blueberries, using only a few strokes and handling the mixture as little as possible.

6. Turn out the dough onto a work surface floured with 1 tablespoon flour. Pat out dough until it is about 1" thick. Cut into 12 pieces in any shape you'd like (I like triangles since it uses most of the dough on the first roll), rerolling the dough as necessary and cutting out the scones until no dough remains. If you'd like to freeze some dough to bake later, wrap pieces individually in plastic wrap and freeze in a freezer-safe storage container up to 2 months. When you're ready to bake at a later date, there is no need to thaw the dough; simply remove plastic wrap and follow normal baking instructions.

7. Place scones on an ungreased baking sheet and bake 25–30 minutes or until tops are golden brown. Let cool on the pan about 10 minutes before serving.

Calories: 150 | Fat: 8g | Protein: 4g | Sodium: 110mg | Fiber: 2g | Carbohydrates: 18g | Sugar: 3g | Added Sugar: 2g

3½ cups plus 1 tablespoon
all-purpose flour, divided

1 tablespoon plus 1 teaspoon
baking powder

1½ tablespoons salt

½ cup granulated sugar

¾ cup unsalted butter

2 large eggs

1¾ cups heavy cream

1 cup shredded Cheddar cheese

CHEDDAR SCONES

This savory scone recipe is considered a cream scone, as it's made using heavy cream in combination with butter. This makes for a moist and soft scone, which most kids prefer over the drier types made with all butter. The dough is a little sticky to roll, but it's well worth the effort.

1. Preheat oven to 350°F.

2. In a large mixing bowl, sift together 3½ cups flour, baking powder, salt, and sugar; mix to combine.

3. Use two knives or your hands to cut the butter into the flour mixture until it's the size of small peas, about 1 minute.

4. In a medium mixing bowl, beat the eggs. Add heavy cream and beat with an electric hand mixer on medium until well combined, about 1 minute.

5. Make a well in the dry ingredients. Pour egg mixture into the center and mix again, about 1 minute.

6. Sprinkle grated cheese over dough and gently fold in until evenly distributed throughout the dough, about 1 minute.

7. Turn out the dough onto a work surface floured with 1 tablespoon flour. Roll out to about 1" thick. Cut into 20 pieces in any shape you like (I like triangles since it uses most of the dough on the first roll), rerolling the dough as necessary and cutting out the scones until no dough remains. If you'd like to freeze some dough to bake later, wrap pieces individually in plastic wrap and freeze in a freezer-safe storage container up to 2 months. When you're ready to bake at a later date, there is no need to thaw the dough; simply remove plastic wrap and follow normal baking instructions.

8. Place scones on an ungreased baking sheet and bake 25–30 minutes or until tops are golden brown. Let cool on the pan about 10 minutes before serving.

Calories: 260 | Fat: 17g | Protein: 5g | Sodium: 50mg | Fiber: 0g | Carbohydrates: 23g | Sugar: 6g | Added Sugar: 5g

CHEESY EGG CUPS

Serves 6
(serving size: 2 egg cups)

PREP: 10 minutes
COOK: 20 minutes

These flavorful and filling egg cups are loaded with vegetables—including zucchini and bell peppers—and provide more than 20 percent of the recommended daily value for protein with no added sugar. Best of all, they can be made ahead of time and then frozen. Simply reheat in the microwave about 1 minute for a quick grab-and-go savory breakfast.

Cooking spray

6 large eggs

½ cup skim milk

¼ teaspoon salt

¼ teaspoon garlic powder

⅛ teaspoon freshly ground black pepper

1 cup shredded Cheddar cheese

½ cup chopped zucchini

½ cup chopped and seeded red bell pepper

1. Preheat oven to 350°F. Grease a 12-cup muffin pan with cooking spray.

2. Beat eggs, milk, salt, garlic powder, and black pepper in a medium bowl until well blended, about 1 minute. Add cheese, zucchini, and bell pepper; mix well another 30 seconds.

3. Spoon the egg mixture into the prepared pan, dividing it equally among the muffin cups (about ¼ cup mixture per cup).

4. Bake about 20 minutes or until just set.

5. Let the pan cool on a wire rack. Remove from muffin cups; serve warm or freeze to enjoy later.

The Incredible Egg

Eggs have thirteen essential nutrients, including high-quality protein. The high-quality protein in eggs is essential for building and maintaining lean body mass, plus it helps you feel full longer—a good quality for any breakfast ingredient.

Calories: 160 | Fat: 11g | Protein: 12g | Sodium: 290mg | Fiber: 0g | Carbohydrates: 4g | Sugar: 2g | Added Sugar: 0g

Chapter 3

DRINKS

Did you know that beverages are the number one source of added sugar in the typical US diet, accounting for almost half of all added sugars consumed in the United States? From soft drinks, fruit drinks, and energy drinks to flavored milks, coffees, and other frothy beverages, there is no shortage of highly sweetened, liquid temptations available these days.

A recent national survey found that almost two-thirds of boys and girls consume at least one sugar-sweetened beverage a day. In fact, studies show that boys drink an average of about 160 calories a day from sugar-sweetened beverages while girls drink about 120 calories a day. This means that most kids exceed the recommended daily limit of added sugars from beverages alone, which doesn't even account for all the added sugars in the foods kids typically eat.

While kids should drink mostly water, making sure that happens is often easier said than done if you're a parent. If sugar-sweetened beverages are a regular thing in your home, simply switching to water and plain milk can immediately cut your child's sugar intake in half. That said, sometimes baby steps are easier, and everyone needs to mix things up. The recipes in this chapter will help you banish beverage boredom while still keeping sugar in check. These drinks can be the perfect solution when you're finding it difficult to keep your child hydrated or when you're celebrating a special occasion.

2 tablespoons lemon juice

1 tablespoon lime juice

½ cup ice cubes

3 slices lemon, cut into
half-moons

2 slices lime, cut into half-moons

12 ounces soda water

LEMON-LIME SODA

Some popular lemon-lime soda brands claim they use natural sugars, but that doesn't make a drink healthy. An 8-ounce serving of traditional lemon-lime soda is loaded with a whopping 25 grams of sugar. Who needs it? Skip the sugar altogether and stir up this crisp, clean version in 2 minutes flat.

1. In a large drinking glass, stir together lemon juice and lime juice.

2. Add ice, then lemon and lime slices to glass, saving 1 lemon half-moon for garnish.

3. Pour soda water into the glass, place remaining lemon half-moon on the rim of glass, and serve.

Calories: 10 | Fat: 0g | Protein: 0g | Sodium: 75mg | Fiber: 0g | Carbohydrates: 3g | Sugar: 1g | Added Sugar: 0g

APPLE SODA

Serves 2

PREP: 5 minutes
COOK: 20 minutes

Inspired by Manzanita Sol, a popular soda in Mexico, this recipe condenses a bit of apple juice into naturally sweet syrup with no sugar added. Unlike the brand-name version, which has 42 grams of sugar per 12-ounce serving, this version has absolutely no added sugar. It's perfect any time of year, but is especially satisfying as the season transitions into autumn.

⅔ cup apple juice

Ice cubes, as needed

2 cups soda water

1. Bring apple juice to a simmer in a small saucepan over medium heat. Reduce heat to low and continue to simmer about 20 minutes, stirring occasionally. Remove from heat when juice becomes syrupy. Let cool.

2. Fill 2 tall glasses with ice. Divide syrup between the glasses. Add soda water, dividing it evenly. Serve immediately.

Calories: 40 | Fat: 0g | Protein: 0g | Sodium: 55mg | Fiber: 0g | Carbohydrates: 9g | Sugar: 8g | Added Sugar: 0g

RUBY RED SODA

Serves 1

PREP: 2 minutes
COOK: N/A

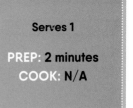

You will love the bright red color of this sparkling soda, especially because it's colored and flavored naturally with hibiscus tea, instead of artificial dyes and sugars. Hibiscus tea is naturally caffeine-free, so is a great option for kids who want a break from plain water. If you can't find hibiscus tea, try passion fruit tea.

½ cup water

2 hibiscus tea bags

½ cup ice cubes

3 thin slices lime

½ cup soda water

1. Bring water to a boil in a small saucepan or tea kettle, then remove from heat and pour into a mug. Add tea bags; steep 5 minutes to create a bright red "condensed" tea.

2. Remove tea bags from mug and let tea cool at least 10 minutes.

3. Pour tea into a tall glass; add ice cubes, 2 slices lime, and soda water. Serve with the remaining lime slice on the rim of the glass.

Calories: 0 | Fat: 0g | Protein: 0g | Sodium: 30mg | Fiber: 0g | Carbohydrates: 0g | Sugar: 0g |
Added Sugar: 0g

RASPBERRY MINT LEMONADE

Think of this as the ultimate kiddie cocktail—a perfect combination of sweet raspberries, refreshing mint, and tart lemon juice. If your kids can't handle pulp, let the drink steep for about 1 hour, then strain before serving. To convert this into an adult beverage, feel free to spike it responsibly.

1 tablespoon honey
3½ cups water, divided
½ pint raspberries
¼ cup fresh mint leaves
⅔ cup lemon juice
Ice cubes, as needed

1. Combine honey and ½ cup water in a small saucepan. Bring to a simmer over medium heat. Reduce heat to low and continue to simmer about 5 minutes, stirring frequently. Remove from heat and let cool.

2. Place raspberries and mint leaves in a small pitcher. Use a wooden spoon to crush until mint is pulpy and raspberries are smashed.

3. Stir in lemon juice, honey water, and remaining water.

4. Refrigerate until cool, about 30 minutes. Serve in tall glasses over ice cubes.

Calories: 40 | Fat: 0g | Protein: 1g | Sodium: 0mg | Fiber: 2g | Carbohydrates: 11g | Sugar: 6g | Added Sugar: 4g

WATERMELON JUICE

Nothing says summer quite like the sweet, juicy taste of watermelon. If anything could possibly be more refreshing than a cool slice of watermelon, it's this freshly made watermelon juice. Even though watermelon is made up of a fair amount of natural sugar, it's also a good source of potassium, vitamin A, and vitamin C, making it a great way to rehydrate on a hot day.

1 small, seedless watermelon (about 6 pounds)

Juice of 1 medium lime

Ice cubes, as needed

1. Cut watermelon into medium-sized chunks, discarding the rind.

2. Blend watermelon in a blender until pulverized, about 2 minutes.

3. Add lime juice to blender and blend another 20 seconds. Serve over ice cubes.

Calories: 200 | Fat: 0g | Protein: 2g | Sodium: 0mg | Fiber: 2g | Carbohydrates: 52g | Sugar: 49g | Added Sugar: 0g

STRAWBERRY SLUSHY

2 cups frozen hulled, sliced strawberries

½ cup ice cubes

Juice of 1 medium lemon

2 teaspoons honey

¾ cup water

4 fresh mint leaves (for garnish)

One day my family and I were on a road trip when a tornado forced us into a gas station for several hours. The gas station had a wall of slushy machines, taunting my kids. Rather than letting them fill up on loads of sugar and artificial colors, I promised we would make our own the next day. This is the result. It's full of flavor, but without all the fake ingredients.

Use a blender to purée all ingredients until they are nice and slushy, about 1 minute, depending on blender power. Pour into serving glasses, garnish each with fresh mint leaves, and serve immediately.

Calories: 80 | Fat: 0g | Protein: 0g | Sodium: 0mg | Fiber: 3g | Carbohydrates: 20g | Sugar: 12g | Added Sugar: 5g

The Vitamin C Booster

Fresh strawberries are often ranked number one as kids' favorite fruit for their naturally sweet taste. That's good news since strawberries are packed with fiber, potassium, and health-promoting phytochemicals. Even better news: strawberries have more vitamin C per serving than oranges, apples, bananas, and grapes!

Serves 6

PREP: 5 minutes
COOK: N/A

½ medium English cucumber, very thinly sliced (unpeeled)

¼ cup roughly chopped fresh mint leaves

1 large lemon, sliced into ¼" rounds

6 cups cold water

CUCUMBER WATER

When you're in the mood for something light and refreshing, this spa-inspired water always does the trick. It's also a great tool for when you or your child are craving something sweet. Simply sip on a tall glass of this revitalizing beverage to reset your mood and your taste buds.

Add all ingredients to a pitcher. Stir well and let sit in refrigerator at least 1 hour to infuse flavors before serving.

Calories: 0 | Fat: 0g | Protein: 0g | Sodium: 0mg | Fiber: 0g | Carbohydrates: 0g | Sugar: 0g | Added Sugar: 0g

THE REHYDRATOR

Serves 2

PREP: 2 minutes
COOK: N/A

When kids are a bit dehydrated, it's nice to give them a quick electrolyte pick-me-up. Unfortunately, most store-bought versions of electrolyte beverages are made with artificial sugars and food dyes. This all-natural version gets its electrolytes from coconut water, a pinch of salt, and a splash of orange juice, which are much better alternatives to the fake stuff.

2 cups coconut water

1 tablespoon orange juice

¼ teaspoon salt

Mix together all ingredients in a pitcher. Serve.

Calories: 45 | Fat: 0g | Protein: 0g | Sodium: 310mg | Fiber: 0g | Carbohydrates: 11g | Sugar: 9g | Added Sugar: 0g

Staying Hydrated

As a general rule, kids ages four through eight should drink at least 5 cups of water a day; kids ages nine through thirteen should have 7–8 cups a day; and kids ages fourteen and older should have 8–13 cups a day. Before, during, and after any physical activity, kids should drink plenty of water, especially in hot weather. The goal is to drink a ½ cup to 2 cups of water every 15–20 minutes while exercising.

HEALTHIER HOT COCOA

Serves 1

PREP: 2 minutes
COOK: 5 minutes

Hot cocoa is a wintertime staple, but if you're cutting back on sugar, it's a definite indulgence. This recipe lowers the sugar by using unsweetened cocoa powder and a spoonful of maple syrup in place of traditional sugary chocolate powders. Flavored with almond milk and almond extract, this chocolate-rich hot cocoa is a comforting and festive treat.

1 cup unsweetened almond milk

2 teaspoons unsweetened cocoa powder

1 teaspoon pure maple syrup

¼ teaspoon pure almond extract

⅛ teaspoon salt

Combine all ingredients in a medium saucepan and simmer over medium heat, stirring frequently. When hot, but before boiling (about 5 minutes), remove from pan and serve in a mug.

Calories: 50 | Fat: 3g | Protein: 1g | Sodium: 440mg | Fiber: 1g | Carbohydrates: 7g | Sugar: 4g | Added Sugar: 4g

6 ounces unsweetened almond
milk
1 decaffeinated chai tea bag
1 teaspoon honey
1 (3") cinnamon stick

ALMOND MILK CHAI LATTE

There's no doubt about it, kids like to mimic their parents. While kids should avoid caffeinated beverages, this Almond Milk Chai Latte gives them the chance to savor in the ritual of a morning cup. Regular chai tea has about one-third the caffeine as a cup of coffee, but to keep your kid caffeine-free, opt for a decaffeinated version.

1. In a mug, heat almond milk in the microwave on high 1–2 minutes until hot but not boiling.

2. Add tea bag, honey, and cinnamon stick. Let steep 5 minutes.

3. Remove tea bag and cinnamon stick. Drink.

Calories: 50 | Fat: 2g | Protein: 1g | Sodium: 140mg | Fiber: 0g | Carbohydrates: 7g | Sugar: 5g | Added Sugar: 5g

Chapter 4

LUNCH

Pulling together a healthful lunch for your child is a worthy goal. While a PB&J on white bread and a bag of cheese puffs may temporarily fill them up, it's not really nourishing kids in the way their bodies need to fuel them throughout the day.

The simple, healthy lunches in this chapter will help you take the panic out of daily lunch-making. With a focus on low-sugar and wholesome variety, these kid-approved recipes take the guesswork out of how to prepare fresh lunches that your kids will actually eat.

As with all the low-sugar meals in this book, there is an emphasis on fresh, whole foods, which are packed with both nutrients and flavor. In general, most kids' lunches are lacking in vegetables, so you'll find lots of ideas in this chapter for how to successfully add those to your child's midday meal.

CONFETTI COUSCOUS SALAD

1½ cups water

1 teaspoon plus ¼ teaspoon salt, divided

1 cup dried whole-wheat pearl couscous

2 medium carrots, peeled and diced

½ medium red bell pepper, seeded and diced

½ medium yellow bell pepper, seeded and diced

1 cup canned garbanzo beans, rinsed and drained

1 (2.25-ounce) can sliced black olives, rinsed and drained

⅓ cup extra-virgin olive oil

2 tablespoons lime juice

½ teaspoon freshly ground black pepper

¼ cup mint leaves, measured then finely chopped

This colorful, refreshing grain salad is on regular rotation in my home. It's a great make-ahead party dish and it packs perfectly in a leakproof container for a school lunch. Make sure you use pearl couscous, also called Israeli couscous. It's bigger in size than regular couscous and has a slightly chewier texture. This recipe calls for the whole-wheat version, but feel free to substitute it for the traditional or tricolored variety.

1. Bring water and ¼ teaspoon salt to a boil in a medium pot. Once boiling, add couscous. Reduce heat to simmer, cover, and cook until water is absorbed, about 10 minutes. Remove from heat and let sit, covered, about 2 minutes. Gently fluff with a fork and transfer to a medium-sized serving bowl. Let cool 5 minutes.

2. Once couscous has cooled, add carrots, bell peppers, garbanzo beans, and olives. Toss so all ingredients are well combined.

3. In a small bowl whisk together olive oil, lime juice, remaining salt, and pepper. Pour over couscous and gently toss until couscous and vegetables are evenly coated.

4. Top with mint and serve at room temperature or store in an airtight container in the refrigerator 3 days.

Calories: 210 | Fat: 11g | Protein: 4g | Sodium: 480mg | Fiber: 2g | Carbohydrates: 24g | Sugar: 2g | Added Sugar: 0g

SESAME SOBA NOODLES

Serves 4

PREP: 5 minutes
COOK: 10 minutes

This cold noodle dish with a simple Asian-inspired vinaigrette comes together in just 10 minutes. You can find soba noodles at most major supermarkets or online grocery retailers, but if you have trouble finding them, feel free to replace the soba noodles with whole-grain linguini. While this recipe is on the mild side, if your family can handle a bit of kick, sprinkle on 1 teaspoon red pepper flakes along with the sesame seeds.

1. Prepare soba noodles according to package directions. Drain, rinse under cold water, and drain again. Transfer noodles to a large serving bowl.

2. In a small mixing bowl, whisk together soy sauce, vinegar, and oil. Pour mixture over noodles and toss. Add cucumbers and sesame seeds; toss again. Serve cold or at room temperature.

Calories: 200 | Fat: 5g | Protein: 8g | Sodium: 490mg | Fiber: 1g | Carbohydrates: 34g | Sugar: 2g | Added Sugar: 0g

6 ounces uncooked soba noodles

1½ tablespoons reduced-sodium soy sauce

1 tablespoon rice vinegar

1 tablespoon toasted sesame oil

1 medium cucumber, peeled, seeded, and sliced into half-moons

2 tablespoons black sesame seeds

About Soba Noodles

Soba noodles are made of buckwheat flour and have a toasty, nutty flavor. Despite its name, buckwheat isn't related to wheat and can be safely enjoyed by those with gluten allergies or sensitivities.

GREEK TORTELLINI SALAD

Serves 8

PREP: **15 minutes**
COOK: **N/A**

This Greek-inspired pasta salad is great for school lunches and also makes for a great picnic or potluck dish. Loaded with fresh vegetables and cheesy tortellini, it's colorful, wholesome, and satisfying. If you don't have tortellini on hand, feel free to use another type of pasta, such as farfalle or fusilli.

1. In a small bowl, whisk together oil, balsamic, salt, and black pepper to make salad dressing.

2. In a large serving bowl, gently toss together tortellini, tomatoes, cucumber, yellow pepper, onion, garbanzo beans, feta, and olives.

3. Pour salad dressing over tortellini and veggies. Toss well to coat. Garnish with mint. Serve immediately or refrigerate up to 3 days.

Calories: 450 | Fat: 25g | Protein: 14g | Sodium: 710mg | Fiber: 2g | Carbohydrates: 44g | Sugar: 5g | Added Sugar: 0g

½ cup extra-virgin olive oil

¼ cup balsamic vinegar

½ teaspoon salt

¼ teaspoon freshly ground black pepper

20 ounces cheese tortellini, cooked according to package instructions

1 pint cherry tomatoes, halved

1 medium cucumber, peeled and diced

1 medium yellow bell pepper, seeded and diced

¼ small red onion, peeled and thinly sliced

1 cup canned garbanzo beans, rinsed and drained

1 cup crumbled feta cheese

½ cup sliced black olives, drained

½ cup roughly chopped fresh mint leaves

Serves 4

PREP: 10 minutes
COOK: N/A

CUCUMBER TEA SANDWICHES

4 ounces cream cheese, softened

3 tablespoons finely chopped fresh dill

1 teaspoon fresh lemon juice

½ teaspoon lemon zest

⅛ teaspoon kosher salt

⅛ teaspoon freshly ground black pepper

8 slices sprouted whole-grain bread

½ medium English cucumber, very thinly sliced (unpeeled)

When done well, cucumber tea sandwiches can be the highlight of an afternoon tea party or playdate. The key is to elevate the spread with simple ingredients, such as fresh dill and lemon zest, as well as firm sprouted bread. When it comes to the cucumber, opt for an English cucumber, also known as a hothouse cucumber. Not only is this type of cucumber seedless, but the skin is thinner and it has a sweeter taste than traditional cucumbers.

1. Place softened cream cheese in a medium bowl. Stir with a fork until smooth and creamy, about 1 minute. Add dill, lemon juice, lemon zest, salt, and pepper; stir until well combined, about 1 minute.

2. Cover bowl with plastic wrap or transfer to an airtight container and chill in refrigerator at least 2 hours. This will allow the flavors to meld.

3. Thirty minutes prior to assembling the sandwiches, remove the cream cheese mixture from the refrigerator to allow it to soften.

4. Lay 4 slices bread on a work space. Spread a thin layer of cream cheese mixture on each slice of bread, dividing it evenly. Arrange cucumber slices on top, dividing them equally. Top with remaining bread slices.

5. Trim off the crusts from the sandwiches with a serrated knife. Cut sandwiches into desired shapes; both triangles and squares look nice. Serve immediately or within 2 hours of being assembled.

Calories: 260 | Fat: 11g | Protein: 10g | Sodium: 160mg | Fiber: 0g | Carbohydrates: 33g | Sugar: 1g | Added Sugar: 0g

HAM AND SWISS PINWHEELS

Serves 8

PREP: **10 minutes**
COOK: **12 minutes**

These buttery, flaky crescent roll-ups are a kid favorite and a crowd-pleaser for laid-back parties. While they feel indulgent, you can keep the nutritionals in check by opting for reduced-fat crescent dough and low-sodium ham. Round out the meal with a simple vegetable tray served with homemade ranch dressing.

Cooking spray

1 (8-ounce) tube reduced-fat crescent roll dough

2 tablespoons Dijon mustard

8 ounces low-sodium sliced ham

8 ounces sliced Swiss cheese

2 tablespoons unsalted butter, melted

¼ teaspoon garlic powder

1. Preheat oven to 350°F. Grease an 8" × 8" baking pan with cooking spray.

2. Unroll crescent dough and cut it evenly into 8 rectangles. Use your fingers to pinch together and smooth any perforations in the dough.

3. Spread mustard onto each rectangle, dividing it evenly. Top with sliced ham and cheese, again dividing evenly. You may need to use a knife to cut the cheese to match the shape of the dough pieces.

4. Starting with the short side of the rectangle, roll up each rectangle and pinch edges to seal. Use a serrated knife to cut each roll into 5 slices. Place cut side up on the prepared baking pan with the rolls just barely touching one another.

5. Pour butter over rolls and sprinkle with garlic powder.

6. Bake 10–12 minutes or until rolls are golden and cheese is melted. Serve warm.

Calories: 270 | Fat: 18g | Protein: 16g | Sodium: 640mg | Fiber: 0g | Carbohydrates: 13g | Sugar: 2g | Added Sugar: 0g

2 slices sprouted whole-grain
bread

2 teaspoons unsalted butter,
divided

2 teaspoons honey mustard,
divided

2 (1-ounce) slices sharp
Cheddar cheese

4 thin slices Granny Smith apple
(unpeeled)

APPLE CHEDDAR MELT

This savory Apple Cheddar Melt take the standard grilled cheese to a whole other level. I like to use sprouted whole-grain bread for this recipe. Sprouting is a process that releases and retains the nutrients stored in whole grains, while also making it easier to digest them. Plus, sprouted whole-grain bread typically has a hearty texture that stands up well to grilling.

1. Heat a large skillet on medium.

2. Spread one side of each slice of bread with 1 teaspoon butter. Spread the other side of each slice with 1 teaspoon honey mustard. Place both slices of bread butter side down in the hot skillet.

3. Place 1 slice cheese on each slice of bread. When the cheese is about halfway melted, about 3 minutes, add the apple slices to one of the slices of bread. Use a spatula to flip the other slice of bread over on top of the other and press lightly.

4. Flip the sandwich a few times in the skillet, pressing gently until the cheese is completely melted and the bread is golden and crispy, about 2 minutes.

Calories: 490 | Fat: 28g | Protein: 21g | Sodium: 450mg | Fiber: 1g | Carbohydrates: 40g | Sugar: 6g | Added Sugar: 0g

2 slices whole-grain bread

2 tablespoons sunflower seed
butter, divided

1 tablespoon Raspberry Jam (see
Chapter 9), divided

SUNFLOWER SEED BUTTER
SUSHI ROLL

The classic PB&J gets a visual upgrade when rolled into these cute little sushi-shaped bites. Any nut or seed butter will do, but I like to use sunflower seed butter to keep it friendly with school allergy policies. This also makes for a great playdate food or after-school snack, especially when served with a tray of fresh-cut fruits and veggies.

1. Cut off crusts from bread and use a rolling pin to flatten bread as thin as possible, about ⅛" or less.

2. Spread 1 tablespoon butter on each slice of bread and top each with ½ tablespoon jam.

3. Roll each slice into a tight spiral. Cut each into 4 pieces and serve immediately.

Calories: 450 | Fat: 21g | Protein: 6g | Sodium: 320mg | Fiber: 2g | Carbohydrates: 55g | Sugar: 15g | Added Sugar: 8g

VEGGIE MONSTER SANDWICH

Serves 1

PREP: 5 minutes
COOK: 2 minutes

This satisfying sandwich is loaded with avocado, spinach, cucumber, tomato, and pesto, making it a hefty, yet healthy, lunch. The fresh mozzarella adds a mild creaminess that is the perfect counterpart to the earthy bread. If you don't have fresh mozzarella, feel free to replace it with part-skim mozzarella slices.

Lightly toast bread. Spread smashed avocado on 1 slice bread and top with mozzarella, spinach, cucumber, and tomato. Smear pesto on remaining slice of bread and place on top to close the sandwich. Use a serrated knife to cut in half and serve immediately.

Calories: 510 | Fat: 27g | Protein: 12g | Sodium: 540mg | Fiber: 3g | Carbohydrates: 45g | Sugar: 7g | Added Sugar: 0g

2 slices whole-grain bread

¼ medium avocado, peeled and gently smashed with a fork

2 (1-ounce) slices fresh mozzarella cheese

⅛ cup baby spinach leaves

6 thin slices English cucumber (unpeeled)

3 thin slices fresh tomato

1 tablespoon pesto

½ cup (4 ounces) reduced-fat garden vegetable cream cheese

4 (9") low-sodium whole-wheat tortillas

½ cup shredded Cheddar cheese

½ cup peeled and shredded carrots

1 (8-ounce) package low-sodium turkey breast slices

TURKEY ROLL-UPS

These Turkey Roll-Ups are a lunchbox favorite and a playdate staple. To make your life just a tad easier, make them up to a day in advance, wrap them individually in plastic wrap, and refrigerate. When you're ready to eat, just remove the plastic wrap, slice, and serve.

1. Spread 2 tablespoons cream cheese over entire surface of each tortilla.

2. Sprinkle 2 tablespoons Cheddar cheese and 2 tablespoons carrots evenly over the surface of each tortilla.

3. Place 2 slices turkey on the bottom half of each tortilla. Roll the tortillas starting at the bottom edge. Wrap in plastic wrap and refrigerate until ready to serve.

4. When ready to serve, remove plastic wrap and use a serrated knife to cut wraps into 1" slices. Arrange slices on a platter and serve.

Calories: 490 | Fat: 16g | Protein: 27g | Sodium: 825mg | Fiber: 0g | Carbohydrates: 56g | Sugar: 0g | Added Sugar: 0g

CHEF SALAD SKEWERS

Serves 8

PREP: 10 minutes
COOK: N/A

There's something about food on a stick that both kids and adults love. These colorful skewers are packed with protein and vegetables. Use any type of skewer you have on hand; I like to use 10" bamboo skewers. Feel free to get creative with how you layer the ingredients on the skewers, alternating colors and textures to keep things interesting. Serve with Quick Ranch Dip (see Chapter 9) or dressing of choice.

1. Thread all ingredients onto 8 skewers, dividing the ingredients equally among the skewers. The following is a suggested pattern, but feel free to get creative: bread cube, tomato, lettuce leaves, ham cube, cucumber round, cheese cube, egg, turkey cube, cucumber round, lettuce leaves, bread cube, tomato.

2. Serve immediately or refrigerate up to 1 day.

Calories: 170 | Fat: 8g | Protein: 15g | Sodium: 380mg | Fiber: 0g | Carbohydrates: 11g | Sugar: 2g |
Added Sugar: 0g

4 thick slices Italian bread, crusts removed, cut into 16 (1½") squares

16 cherry tomatoes

4 large Boston lettuce leaves, roughly trimmed into 2" squares

4 ounces low-sodium ham, cut into cubes

1 medium cucumber, peeled and sliced into 16 rounds

4 ounces Swiss cheese, cut into cubes

4 hard-boiled eggs, shelled and cut in half

4 ounces low-sodium smoked turkey, cut into cubes

VEGETABLE SPRING ROLLS

Serves 5
(serving size: 2 spring rolls)

PREP: 15 minutes
COOK: N/A

These spring rolls make for a refreshing, satisfying lunch. Like a mini self-contained salad, they are perfect for little hands. This is also a perfect recipe for budding chefs to expand on their kitchen skills; from soaking the rice paper to piling the ingredients onto the softened rice paper, even the youngest of kids can help. Serve with Spicy Peanut Dip (see Chapter 9).

2 cups warm water

10 large rice paper wrappers

1 medium red bell pepper, seeded and cut into thin strips about 3" long

1 medium cucumber, peeled and cut into thin strips about 3" long

1 large carrot, peeled and cut into thin strips about 3" long

1 medium avocado, peeled, seeded, and cut into ¼" slices

1 cup stemmed fresh mint leaves, divided

1. Fill a shallow dish with warm water. Submerge 1 spring roll wrapper in water about 20 seconds until slightly softened.

2. Lay softened wrapper on a work service. Place 3 red pepper strips, 3 cucumber strips, 3 carrot strips, 2 avocado slices, and about 1½ tablespoons mint in the lower-middle portion of the wrapper. Fold sides of wrapper over the filling and roll it up.

3. Repeat with remaining ingredients, dividing them equally among the wrappers. Serve immediately or wrap individually in plastic wrap and refrigerate up to 24 hours.

Calories: 130 | Fat: 4.5g | Protein: 4g | Sodium: 30mg | Fiber: 3g | Carbohydrates: 20g | Sugar: 3g | Added Sugar: 0g

Customize Your Rolls

Let everyone in your family choose their own fillings to customize their spring roll. Beyond the ingredients listed in this recipe, you can choose from grilled chicken, shrimp, or tofu slices, cellophane noodles, cream cheese, radish slices, and more!

2 tablespoons canola oil, divided

¼ cup finely chopped white onion

1 (15-ounce) can low-sodium black beans, drained and rinsed

1 (15-ounce) can unsalted corn, drained and rinsed

2 teaspoons light brown sugar

¼ cup salsa

8 (6") corn tortillas

1 cup shredded Monterey jack cheese, divided

BLACK BEAN AND SWEET CORN QUESADILLAS

These scrumptious quesadillas are a little bit sweet and a little bit spicy. Like all other legumes, black beans are prized for their high protein and fiber content, making them a good plant-based food to regularly incorporate into your family's diet. For a touch of creaminess, serve these quesadillas with a side of sour cream and guacamole.

1. Add 1 tablespoon oil to a large skillet and heat on medium. Stir in onion and cook until softened, about 3 minutes, stirring frequently.

2. Add beans, corn, brown sugar, and salsa to skillet; mix well. Continue to cook over medium heat, stirring occasionally, about 5 minutes. Transfer mixture to a medium bowl. Remove skillet from heat and use a paper towel to gently wipe skillet clean.

3. Return skillet to stovetop. Use a pastry brush to lightly coat one side of each tortilla with remaining oil, dividing it evenly among them. Place 1 tortilla oiled side down in skillet and sprinkle with ¼ cup cheese and roughly ¾ cup of the bean mixture. Top with another tortilla, oiled side up.

4. Cook until golden, about 2 minutes, then flip and cook on the other side until golden, about 2 minutes. Repeat with remaining tortillas and filling.

5. Once all quesadillas have been assembled and cooked, use a serrated knife to cut each into quarters and serve.

Calories: 460 | Fat: 18g | Protein: 17g | Sodium: 440mg | Fiber: 9g | Carbohydrates: 59g | Sugar: 7g | Added Sugar: 2g

SWEET POTATO AND SPINACH QUESADILLAS

Serves 4

PREP: 10 minutes
COOK: 30 minutes

These quesadillas are a perfect blend of sweet and spice, melded together by creamy sweet potatoes and gooey cheese. To help speed up your prep time, you can prepare the sweet potato filling a day in advance, then simply assemble and grill the quesadillas right before you're ready to serve. These also freeze well. After grilling them, leave them uncut and let them cool, then transfer to a zip-top bag with parchment paper layered between each quesadilla to prevent them from sticking.

2 medium sweet potatoes

1 teaspoon ground cumin

½ teaspoon ground cinnamon

¼ teaspoon freshly ground black pepper

8 (8") whole-wheat tortillas

1 tablespoon olive oil

4 cups baby spinach leaves

1 cup shredded part-skim mozzarella

1. Place sweet potatoes on a microwave-safe plate. Microwave on high until tender, about 15 minutes.

2. Let potatoes cool slightly, about 5 minutes, then use a serrated knife to cut them in half. Use a spoon to scoop out the flesh. Discard the skin.

3. Use a fork to mash the potato flesh. Sprinkle in cumin, cinnamon, and pepper, continuing to mash until well combined. You should have about 1 cup sweet potato filling.

4. Heat a large skillet on medium. Use a pastry brush to lightly coat one side of each tortilla with oil, dividing it evenly among the tortillas. Place 1 tortilla oiled side down in skillet. Use a fork to spread about ¼ cup sweet potato filling on top of tortilla. Top with 1 cup spinach and ¼ cup mozzarella. Cover with another tortilla, oiled side up.

5. Cook until golden, about 2 minutes, then flip and cook on the other side until golden, another 2 minutes. Repeat with remaining tortillas and filling.

6. Once all quesadillas have been assembled and cooked, use a serrated knife to cut each into quarters and serve.

The Naturally Sweet Potato

Sweet potatoes, like their name implies, are naturally sweet, making them a great food to eat when you're cutting back on added sugars. Sweet potatoes are packed with nutrients, including fiber, potassium, vitamin A, vitamin C, and vitamin B_6, which gives your body a natural energy boost.

Calories: 450 | Fat: 16g | Protein: 17g | Sodium: 910mg | Fiber: 4g | Carbohydrates: 61g | Sugar: 3g | Added Sugar: 0g

PEPPERONI PANZANELLA

This is one of my favorite ways to use the last of a whole-grain bread loaf, just before it goes stale. It's also a favorite family picnic item. We'll pack this into a cooler, along with a few other simple salad dishes and fresh fruit, and be on our way.

2 (1"-thick) slices crusty whole-grain bread, cut into ½" pieces

1 pint cherry tomatoes, halved

8 ounces fresh mozzarella pearls

4 ounces sliced pepperoni, halved

¼ cup extra-virgin olive oil

2 tablespoons red wine vinegar

½ teaspoon kosher salt

¼ teaspoon freshly ground black pepper

1 cup thinly sliced fresh basil leaves

1. Preheat oven to 350°F. Place bread on a baking sheet and toast 10 minutes or until lightly golden. Transfer to a large serving bowl and let cool 5 minutes.

2. Add tomatoes, mozzarella, pepperoni, olive oil, vinegar, salt, and pepper to bowl. Toss to combine. Let sit about 30 minutes to allow bread to soften. Garnish with basil and serve.

Calories: 380 | Fat: 32g | Protein: 14g | Sodium: 570mg | Fiber: 1g | Carbohydrates: 9g | Sugar: 2g | Added Sugar: 0g

BAKED FALAFEL BITES

This twist on traditional falafel is a great source of vegetarian protein, perfect for Meatless Mondays. In addition to the chickpeas, the hemp seeds add an extra boost of protein. While falafel is traditionally deep-fried, this baked version is lighter and lower in fat. Round out the dish by serving it with pita, hummus, hot sauce, lettuce, sliced cucumber, and chopped tomatoes and let everyone in your family assemble their own falafel sandwich.

1 (15-ounce) can low-sodium chickpeas, rinsed, drained, and thoroughly patted dry

½ medium white onion, peeled and chopped

2 cloves garlic, minced

½ cup chopped fresh flat-leaf Italian parsley

¼ cup chopped fresh mint

2 tablespoons hemp seeds

¼ teaspoon freshly ground black pepper

1 teaspoon ground cumin

1 teaspoon baking powder

¼ cup whole-wheat flour

1. Add chickpeas, onion, garlic, parsley, mint, hemp seeds, pepper, and cumin to the bowl of a food processor. Pulse until blended but not puréed, about 1–2 minutes, scraping down the sides of the bowl as needed.

2. Sprinkle in baking powder and flour and continue to pulse until the dough is no longer wet and you can form it into a ball, about 1 minute.

3. Transfer chickpea mixture to a medium bowl, cover, and refrigerate 2 hours so it firms up and is easier to handle.

4. Preheat oven to 400°F. Line a baking sheet with parchment paper.

5. Remove chickpea mixture from refrigerator. Use a tablespoon to scoop out rounded amounts and use your hands to form 12 small disks.

6. Place bites on the prepared baking sheet and bake until golden brown, about 7–10 minutes. Serve immediately.

Frying Falafel

If you'd like to fry falafel the traditional way, fill a deep saucepan with enough oil to come about 3" up of the sides of the pan. Heat the oil to 350°F, using a thermometer to check the temperature. Then deep-fry the falafel in batches until well browned and cooked through, about 4 minutes. Remove from oil and place on a paper towel to soak up any extra oil before serving.

Calories: 170 | Fat: 4.5g | Protein: 9g | Sodium: 150mg | Fiber: 7g | Carbohydrates: 24g | Sugar: 4g | Added Sugar: 0g

Chapter 5

SNACKS

Snacks can be part of a healthy eating plan, especially when you are smart about what you serve and when you serve them. Unfortunately, many packaged snacks are high in sugar, salt, and other highly processed ingredients. While these snacks may be convenient, they're not doing anyone any favors.

Ideally, the foods you serve as snacks should be just as healthy as the foods you serve at meals. The best snack options are real foods, such as fruits, vegetables, nuts, and seeds, which help boost energy, stabilize blood sugar, improve moods, and fill nutritional gaps in your child's diet. Not only do these types of snacks help your child power through from one meal to the next, but they can also take a little pressure off meals. When you know your child is meeting his or her nutrient needs at snack time, you'll be less stressed if the dinner's vegetable choice goes untouched.

The snacks in this chapter, like all the recipes in this book, feature a variety of nourishing whole foods in kid-friendly formats that are sure to up your snack game. To optimize appetites and energy levels, offer young kids a snack about 2 hours after a meal and older kids about 3 hours after a meal.

Serves 24
(serving size: 1 cracker)

PREP: 25 minutes
COOK: 15 minutes

½ cup unsalted butter, softened

⅓ cup honey

⅓ cup packed light brown sugar

2 cups whole-wheat flour

1 cup plus 2 tablespoons
all-purpose flour, divided

¾ teaspoon baking powder

½ teaspoon baking soda

1 teaspoon ground cinnamon

2 teaspoons pure vanilla extract

½ cup unsweetened almond milk

GRAHAM CRACKERS

Graham crackers are practically a staple for kids, but they have more added sugar than you might think. Homemade graham crackers are surprisingly easy to make and even more delicious than the store-bought kind. This recipe creates crackers with a slightly cake-like texture, but if you want a crispier graham you can simply roll out the dough thinner than recommended.

1. In a mixer with a paddle attachment on low speed, cream the butter, honey, and sugar until just combined, about 1 minute. Use a spatula to scrape dough down sides of bowl and mix again, about 1 more minute. The mix does not need to get too fluffy, just completely mixed together.

2. Add whole-wheat flour, 1 cup all-purpose flour, baking powder, baking soda, and cinnamon to the mixer and allow dough to come together on low speed, about 2 minutes.

3. Add vanilla and almond milk to batter and mix again until a smooth dough has formed, about 1 minute. Use a spatula to scrape dough onto a sheet of plastic wrap. Wrap dough and refrigerate at least 3 hours or overnight (cold dough is much easier to roll out).

4. Preheat oven to 350°F. Line a baking sheet with foil.

5. Once dough is chilled, sprinkle 2 tablespoons flour onto a work surface to prevent dough from sticking. Flip dough onto work surface and use a rolling pin to flatten dough to a smooth circle ⅛" thick. Use a pizza cutter wheel to cut the dough into 3" squares or any other desired shape (you can even use shaped cookie cutters to make fun graham crackers). Place the dough on the prepared baking sheet about 1" apart. Use a fork to prick each graham cracker to help keep them from rising.

6. Bake 10–15 minutes. Let cool on the baking sheet about 30 minutes, then wrap completely and store up to 3 weeks at room temperature.

Calories: 130 | Fat: 4g | Protein: 3g | Sodium: 45mg | Fiber: 1g | Carbohydrates: 23g | Sugar: 7g | Added Sugar: 7g

CHEESE CRACKERS

Serves 4
(serving size: 10 crackers)

PREP: 10 minutes
COOK: 12 minutes

When the munchies hit, don't reach for a box of boring store-bought crackers. Instead, try these crispy homemade Cheese Crackers made with whole-wheat flour and sharp Cheddar cheese. This snack will satiate your family's cravings without all the unhealthy additives typically found in boxed versions. These crackers can be stored in an airtight container up to 1 week.

¾ cup white whole-wheat flour

1 cup shredded sharp Cheddar cheese

¼ cup unsalted butter

¼ teaspoon salt

⅛ teaspoon ground cayenne pepper

¼ teaspoon garlic powder

1. Preheat oven to 350°F. Line a baking sheet with parchment paper. Place another sheet of parchment paper on your work surface.

2. In the bowl of a mixer, combine all ingredients on low speed until the dough stars to come together, about 2 minutes.

3. Gather dough into a rough ball and transfer to parchment-covered work surface. Roll dough into a log that is roughly 8" long by 1½" in diameter. Wrap log in plastic wrap and chill in freezer 30 minutes.

4. Remove from freezer and use a serrated knife to slice log cross-wise into about ⅛" rounds, yielding about 40 rounds total. Place on parchment-lined baking sheet, leaving ½" space between each round.

5. Bake 10–12 minutes or until just beginning to brown. Let cool 5 minutes on baking sheet, then transfer to racks to cool completely, about 30 minutes. Store in an airtight container up to a week.

Calories: 280 | Fat: 21g | Protein: 10g | Sodium: 330mg | Fiber: 2g | Carbohydrates: 18g | Sugar: 0g | Added Sugar: 0g

WHOLE-GRAIN PRETZEL BITES

Serves 8
(serving size: 6 bites)

PREP: 20 minutes
COOK: 24 minutes

These mini pretzel bites are a comforting snack when the afternoon munchies hit. While best fresh, you can store them in an airtight container for 3–4 days; just reheat in the microwave about 30 seconds before serving. Serve with homemade Honey Mustard Dip (see Chapter 9).

1½ cups warm water (110–115°F)

1 tablespoon honey

1 (0.25-ounce) package active dry yeast

¼ cup unsalted butter, melted

1 teaspoon salt

2½ cups all-purpose flour

2 cups whole-wheat flour

2 teaspoons vegetable oil, divided

8 cups cold water

½ cup baking soda

1 large egg, beaten with 1 tablespoon cold water

1 tablespoon coarse sea salt

1. In the bowl of a stand mixer, combine warm water, honey, and yeast. Let yeast proof 5 minutes or until a bubbly foam begins to form.

2. Add butter, salt, and flours. Using dough hook, mix on low until dough begins to come together, about 2 minutes. Increase speed to medium-low and mix until dough is smooth, about 5 minutes.

3. Remove dough from bowl, clean the bowl, and oil it with 1 teaspoon vegetable oil. Form dough into a ball and return it to the bowl. Cover with plastic wrap and let sit in a dry, warm place 50 minutes or until dough doubles in size.

4. Preheat oven to 425°F. Line two baking sheets with parchment paper.

5. In a large pot, mix 8 cups cold water and baking soda; bring to a rolling boil.

6. Spread remaining teaspoon vegetable oil on a work surface. Punch down dough and roll out into a log about 1' long. Cut log into 8 equal sections. Roll out each section into a rope and cut each rope into 6 bite-sized pieces, for a total of 48 pieces.

7. Drop 6 pretzel bites at a time into boiling water; boil 30 seconds. Use a slotted spoon to remove and set on a plate lined with paper towels. Repeat with remaining pretzel bites.

8. Transfer pretzel bites to the prepared baking sheets, spaced 1" apart. Brush each pretzel bite with egg wash and top with coarse salt.

9. Bake 15 minutes or until golden brown. Let cool about 5 minutes before serving.

Calories: 320 | Fat: 8g | Protein: 9g | Sodium: 1,170mg | Fiber: 3g | Carbohydrates: 54g | Sugar: 2g | Added Sugar: 2g

8 medium apples, peeled, cored, and chopped into 1" pieces

2 (3") cinnamon sticks

⅛ teaspoon ground ginger

¼ teaspoon salt

1 tablespoon lemon juice

½ cup water

SLOW COOKER APPLESAUCE

Homemade applesauce is an entirely different taste experience than canned applesauce. It's a total flavor bomb explosion in your mouth! You can use any apple variety you want, but I've found that Fuji is a great choice because it's naturally sweet and it breaks down more easily when cooked.

1. Combine all ingredients in the bowl of a slow cooker and stir to combine.

2. Close the lid of the slow cooker and cook on high 4 hours, stirring the applesauce every hour.

3. After 4 hours of cooking, remove the cinnamon sticks and use an immersion blender to purée the applesauce until smooth.

4. Transfer applesauce to 8 small mason jars. Store in the refrigerator 1 week or freeze up to 3 months.

Calories: 100 | Fat: 0g | Protein: 0g | Sodium: 75mg | Fiber: 4g | Carbohydrates: 25g | Sugar: 19g | Added Sugar: 0g

CRAN-APPLE PLATE

Serves 1

PREP: 5 minutes
COOK: N/A

I'm a big fan of taking tried-and-true flavor combos and serving them in the simplest way possible. This simple snack plate is naturally sweet, vividly colorful, and has a great crunch factor, making it an instant hit in my household. Any apples will do, but we're big fans of Ambrosia apples, which are one of the sweetest apple varieties.

1 medium Ambrosia apple with peel on

2 tablespoons lightly sweetened dried cranberries

2 tablespoons walnut pieces

Slice apple into quarters and cut out the core. Dice apple quarters into ½" cubes and put in a bowl. Sprinkle with dried cranberries and walnut pieces. Serve with a spoon for a simple, tasty afternoon snack.

Calories: 240 | Fat: 10g | Protein: 3g | Sodium: 0mg | Fiber: 6g | Carbohydrates: 40g | Sugar: 30g | Added Sugar: 2g

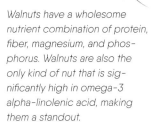

Go Nuts for Walnuts

Walnuts have a wholesome nutrient combination of protein, fiber, magnesium, and phosphorus. Walnuts are also the only kind of nut that is significantly high in omega-3 alpha-linolenic acid, making them a standout.

APPLE PEANUT BUTTER RINGS

Serves 2

PREP: 5 minutes
COOK: N/A

Looking for the ease of a sandwich without all the bread? These wholesome "sandwiches" are a great breadless alternative, featuring juicy apples with a satisfying smear of creamy natural peanut butter. Feel free to use any type of apple, but Granny Smith and Ambrosia both work well because of their crisp and firm texture.

1 medium Granny Smith apple, cored and cut into 8 rings (about ¼" thick), unpeeled

¼ cup natural creamy peanut butter

¼ cup granola

2 tablespoons raisins

Lay apple rings peel side down on a work surface. Spread each with equal amounts peanut butter and top with granola and raisins. Serve immediately.

Calories: 340 | Fat: 17g | Protein: 9g | Sodium: 110mg | Fiber: 5g | Carbohydrates: 35g | Sugar: 19g | Added Sugar: 3g

Topping Inspiration

I've made these in school classrooms many times, with the students as the chefs. Great nut-free creamy alternatives include sunflower seed butter and cream cheese. Other topping ideas include sunflower seeds, chocolate chips, dried cranberries, and coconut. Little hands will likely need help spreading the creamy ingredients but love to hand-pick their toppings.

1½ cups diced peaches
1½ cups diced mango
½ cup water

PEACH MANGO FRUIT LEATHER

These fruit leathers are every bit as fun as fruit roll-ups, but without the artificial dyes and sugar. They're also easy to make. Get creative and experiment with different fruit varieties, such as strawberries, apple, watermelon, pineapple, or cherry. Store in an airtight container at room temperature 1–2 weeks.

1. Preheat oven to 175°F (or lowest temperature). Line a baking sheet with parchment paper.

2. Add fruit to food processor and pulse until partially blended.

3. Pour half the water in and pulse again until only a few chunks remain. Add the remaining water and pulse until completely smooth, about 2 minutes.

4. Transfer fruit purée to the prepared baking sheet and smooth out until surface is even. Bake 3½ hours or until surface is glassy and dry.

5. Remove from pan and cut into 10 strips while still on parchment paper, being sure to also cut through the parchment paper, which will keep the roll-up from sticking to itself as you roll it. Tightly roll each strip, as if you would roll a rug, with the parchment paper on the outside. Tie with a small piece of string and place in an airtight container up to a week.

Calories: 50 | Fat: 0g | Protein: 1g | Sodium: 0mg | Fiber: 1g | Carbohydrates: 12g | Sugar: 10g | Added Sugar: 0g

GRANOLA CUP SUNDAE

Serves 8

PREP: 10 minutes
COOK: 15 minutes

These cute little whole-grain granola cups are topped with yogurt and fresh blueberries for a fun and healthy sundae. I like to save some granola cups in an airtight container for up to a week to make it easy to whip together a healthy after-school snack. In addition to blueberries, strawberries, raspberries, dried cranberries, and pitted cherries all make for tasty toppings.

Cooking spray

1½ cups rolled oats

¼ cup chopped walnuts

½ teaspoon ground cinnamon

½ teaspoon ground nutmeg

¼ teaspoon kosher salt

2 tablespoons honey

2 tablespoons natural creamy peanut butter

1 large egg white

2 cups plain low-fat Greek yogurt

2 cups fresh blueberries

1. Preheat oven to 325°F. Grease an 8-cup muffin pan with cooking spray.

2. Combine oats, walnuts, cinnamon, nutmeg, and salt in a medium bowl.

3. Combine honey and peanut butter in a small microwave-safe bowl. Microwave 20 seconds on high, stirring until smooth.

4. Add honey mixture and egg white to oat mixture; mix until well blended, about 1 minute.

5. Add oat mixture to the prepared muffin pan, dividing it evenly among the muffin cups. Press the mixture into the bottom of each cup, and then make a divot in the center of each and push the mixture firmly around the sides of the muffin cups.

6. Bake 15 minutes or until edges are browned and crisp. Let cool completely, about 30 minutes.

7. Remove granola cups from muffin pan. Fill each granola cup with ¼ cup yogurt and top each with ¼ cup blueberries. Serve immediately.

Calories: 190 | Fat: 7g | Protein: 10g | Sodium: 130mg | Fiber: 7g | Carbohydrates: 24g | Sugar: 10g | Added Sugar: 4g

¼ cup part-skim ricotta cheese

1 slice whole-grain bread, toasted

4 large strawberries, hulled and sliced

½ tablespoon honey

3 fresh basil leaves, cut into thin strips

⅛ teaspoon sea salt

⅛ teaspoon freshly ground black pepper

STRAWBERRY BASIL RICOTTA TOAST

Ripe, juicy strawberries and fresh basil pair perfectly with creamy ricotta for this simple, nourishing summer snack. But don't be deceived by the recipe's simplicity; this toast is worthy enough to serve at a grown-up party; simply double or triple the recipe, cut the toast into triangles or squares, and serve on a pretty platter for a show-stopping festive app.

Spread ricotta on bread. Top with strawberries, drizzle with honey, and then sprinkle with basil, salt, and pepper. Enjoy immediately.

Calories: 200 | Fat: 7g | Protein: 12g | Sodium: 480mg | Fiber: 2g | Carbohydrates: 24g | Sugar: 6g | Added Sugar: 0g

CHOCOLATE PEANUT BUTTER PROTEIN BARS

Serves 8
(serving size: 1 bar)

PREP: 10 minutes
COOK: N/A

Forget store-bought granola bars: these Chocolate Peanut Butter Protein Bars are perfect for a rushed morning. They're small, easy to pack, and thanks to the addition of satiety-boosting protein powder, they'll keep your stomach from rumbling until lunch. You can store these bars in an airtight container in the refrigerator up to 1 week.

PROTEIN BARS

¼ cup natural creamy peanut butter

3 tablespoons coconut oil

3 tablespoons honey

1 teaspoon unsweetened almond milk

6 tablespoons chocolate protein powder

1½ tablespoons unsweetened cocoa powder

2 cups puffed brown rice cereal

PEANUT BUTTER DRIZZLE

1 tablespoon natural creamy peanut butter

2 tablespoons unsweetened almond milk

1. Line an 8" × 8" rimmed baking pan with parchment paper and set aside.

2. To make the bars, stir together peanut butter, coconut oil, honey, and almond milk in a small microwave-safe bowl. Microwave on high about 10 seconds or until runny.

3. Add protein powder and cocoa powder; stir to combine. Use a rubber spatula to mix in rice cereal. Press mixture into the prepared pan and freeze 25 minutes.

4. In a small bowl, create the drizzle by whisking together peanut butter and almond milk until runny and shiny.

5. Cut into 8 bars with a sharp knife and drizzle with peanut butter topping.

Calories: 180 | Fat: 11g | Protein: 5g | Sodium: 95mg | Fiber: 1g | Carbohydrates: 16g | Sugar: 7g | Added Sugar: 6g

CUCUMBER BOATS

6 Persian cucumbers (unpeeled)

12 ounces cream cheese, room temperature

2 teaspoons honey

⅛ teaspoon garlic powder

⅛ teaspoon salt

2 tablespoons walnut pieces

There is something about the combination of cucumbers and cream cheese that is so light and refreshing. Serve these Cucumber Boats on a platter for a birthday party appetizer or playdate snack. They are perfectly pretty as is, but for added pizazz, top with shredded carrot, dried cranberries, or pomegranate seeds.

1. Slice cucumbers in half lengthwise. Use a small melon baller or spoon to scoop out seeds; discard. Place cucumbers cut side down on a paper towel for 1 hour to let water drain out.

2. Place cream cheese and honey in small microwave-safe bowl. Microwave 10 seconds on high to soften. Add garlic powder and salt. Stir well.

3. Scoop cream cheese mixture into a piping bag with a large star tip. Alternatively, scoop into a large zip-top bag and cut a ¼" off bottom corner. Pipe about 1 ounce into each cucumber half, dividing evenly between the 12 halves. Sprinkle with walnut pieces and serve.

Calories: 110 | Fat: 10g | Protein: 2g | Sodium: 115mg | Fiber: 0g | Carbohydrates: 5g | Sugar: 2g | Added Sugar: 1g

Serves 4
(serving size: 2 bites)

PREP: 15 minutes
COOK: N/A

½ cup rolled oats

2 tablespoons water

½ cup lightly sweetened dried cranberries

4 pitted, chopped Medjool dates

¼ cup chopped walnuts

CRANBERRY DATE ENERGY BITES

These little energy bites are a perfect solution when a sugar craving hits. Sweetened and held together by naturally sweet Medjool dates, these energy bites can quickly take the edge of hunger, especially when you're on the go. They can be stored in an airtight container in the refrigerator up to 2 weeks.

1. Place all ingredients in a food processor. Pulse until a crumbly mixture has formed, about 2 minutes.

2. Scoop 1 tablespoon of the mixture into your palm and squeeze together to form a ball. Flatten the ball into a sphere. Repeat with the remaining mixture to form about 8 bites.

3. Place all bites on a cookie sheet lined with parchment paper. Refrigerate at least 15 minutes before serving.

Calories: 160 | Fat: 6g | Protein: 3g | Sodium: 0mg | Fiber: 3g | Carbohydrates: 28g | Sugar: 17g | Added Sugar: 2g

CHOCOLATE BROWNIE PROTEIN BITES

Serves 6
(serving size: 2 bites)

PREP: 10 minutes
COOK: N/A

These dessert-like protein bites are a no-bake, no-hassle, one-bite power snack. Thanks to the addition of protein powder, just 1 bite provides nearly 15 percent of daily protein recommendations, making these a great option for kids who aren't big protein eaters. They can be stored in an airtight container in the refrigerator up to 2 weeks.

¼ cup oat flour

¼ cup unsweetened cocoa powder

½ cup chocolate protein powder

3 tablespoons honey

2 tablespoons unsweetened almond butter

3 tablespoons unsweetened almond milk

1. In a large bowl, sift together oat flour, cocoa powder, and protein powder.

2. Add honey, almond butter, and almond milk; mix with a rubber spatula until a thick, crumbly paste forms, about 2 minutes.

3. Scoop 1 tablespoon of the mixture into your palm and squeeze together to form a ball. Flatten the ball into a sphere. Repeat with the remaining batter to form about 12 bites.

4. Place all bites on a baking sheet lined with parchment paper. Refrigerate at least 20 minutes before serving.

Calories: 120 | Fat: 4.5g | Protein: 7g | Sodium: 80mg | Fiber: 2g | Carbohydrates: 17g | Sugar: 10g | Added Sugar: 8g

STRAWBERRY COCONUT ENERGY BITES

Serves 12
(serving size: 2 bites)

PREP: 15 minutes
COOK: N/A

Freeze-dried fruit has nearly the same nutritional profile as fresh fruit, but with more ease and convenience. This recipe takes advantage of freeze-dried strawberries to create a bright, naturally sweet coating for these energy bites, without needing any artificial colors. They can be stored in an airtight container in the refrigerator up to 2 weeks.

1 cup almond butter

1 cup rolled oats

½ cup unsweetened shredded coconut

½ cup ground flaxseed

⅓ cup honey

2 cups freeze-dried strawberries

1. Combine almond butter, oats, coconut, flaxseed, and honey in a large bowl; beat with a mixer on low until combined, about 2 minutes.

2. Roll mixture into 24 (1") balls and place on a baking sheet lined with parchment paper. Refrigerate about 30 minutes or until firm.

3. Pulse strawberries in a food processor or high-powered blender until powdery, about 30 seconds. Roll the balls in the strawberry powder. Refrigerate in an airtight container until ready to serve.

Calories: 290 | Fat: 17g | Protein: 8g | Sodium: 55mg | Fiber: 6g | Carbohydrates: 33g | Sugar: 23g | Added Sugar: 7g

Benefits of Flaxseed

Flaxseed has been cultivated for centuries and has a reputation for being a powerful little seed and there is research to back this claim. There is evidence that flaxseed, which is high in fiber and omega-3 fatty acids, may help prevent heart disease and certain types of cancer.

1 cup rolled oats

¼ cup ground flaxseed

½ teaspoon ground cinnamon

½ cup natural creamy peanut butter

2 tablespoons pure maple syrup

¼ cup raisins

OATMEAL COOKIE ENERGY BITES

These little energy bites have all the flavor of a classic oatmeal cookie, but with a fraction of the sugar. Enjoy one with a sliced apple for a satisfying after-school snack or pack a few in an insulated bag for an after-sport pick-me-up. These energy bites are best stored in an airtight container in the refrigerator up to 1 week.

1. In a large bowl, mix together oats, flaxseed, and cinnamon; set aside.

2. In a small bowl, mix together peanut butter and maple syrup.

3. Add peanut butter mixture to oat mixture and mix with a rubber spatula until well combined, about 1–2 minutes.

4. Add raisins and mix again. Scoop 1 tablespoon of the batter into your palm and squeeze together to form a ball. Flatten the ball into a sphere. Repeat with the remaining mixture to form about 16 bites.

5. Place all bites on a baking sheet lined with parchment paper. Refrigerate at least 20 minutes before serving.

Calories: 190 | Fat: 10g | Protein: 6g | Sodium: 55mg | Fiber: 3g | Carbohydrates: 18g | Sugar: 7g | Added Sugar: 3g

TRAIL MIX

Trail mix is practically a kid staple, but most store-bought mixes are loaded with sugary add-ins and artificial colors. The key to building a kid-friendly trail mix is to include an equal balance between nuts and "fun stuff," like whole-grain cereal and a small amount of dried fruit and dark chocolate. Package this in small containers for a grab-and-go, travel-friendly snack.

Combine all ingredients in a large bowl and mix well. Store in an airtight container up to 1 month.

Calories: 210 | Fat: 16g | Protein: 6g | Sodium: 55mg | Fiber: 2g | Carbohydrates: 13g | Sugar: 7g | Added Sugar: 5g

½ cup dry-roasted unsalted almonds

½ cup dry-roasted unsalted peanuts

½ cup dry-roasted unsalted pecans

½ cup dried raw pumpkin seeds

½ cup puffed millet cereal

½ cup whole-grain oat cereal, such as Cheerios

½ cup dark chocolate chips

½ cup lightly sweetened dried cranberries

¼ teaspoon sea salt

½ teaspoon ground cinnamon

¼ teaspoon ground nutmeg

CRISPY CINNAMON-DUSTED CHICKPEAS

1 (15-ounce) can low-sodium chickpeas, drained, rinsed, and dried

1 tablespoon canola oil

1 tablespoon granulated sugar

1 tablespoon ground cinnamon

1 teaspoon sea salt

The Vegetable with More

As a legume, chickpeas are considered both a vegetable and a protein food. They are a good source of fiber and plant-based protein, as well as a good vegetarian source of iron. Chickpeas are also rich in folate, which is especially important for women of childbearing age.

These addictively crispy chickpeas strike the perfect balance between sweet and salty. Make sure you remove as much moisture as possible from the chickpeas after rinsing them to maximize the crunch factor. Use paper towels to fully dry them off and squeeze out any remaining water before tossing them with the seasonings.

1. Preheat oven to 400°F.

2. In a medium bowl, toss chickpeas with oil, sugar, and cinnamon. Spread onto a large, rimmed baking sheet and roast in oven. Roughly every 15 minutes, quickly remove the baking sheet from the oven and give it a good shake to ensure the chickpeas roast evenly. Roast a total of 45 minutes or until chickpeas are golden brown and crunchy.

3. Remove chickpeas from oven and sprinkle with salt. Let cool completely before serving or storing in an airtight container up to 3 days.

Calories: 140 | Fat: 6g | Protein: 5g | Sodium: 810mg | Fiber: 6g | Carbohydrates: 19g | Sugar: 6g | Added Sugar: 3g

CORN BREAD MINI MUFFINS

Corn bread is incredibly versatile: it's great with jelly for breakfast or snack time and it also makes a great side for lunch or dinner. This recipe is made with honey and almond flour, which adds a more complex flavor to a traditional classic. You can store these muffins in an airtight container up to 3 days or freeze them up to 1 month.

½ cup all-purpose flour

½ cup almond flour

1 cup cornmeal

1 teaspoon baking soda

1 teaspoon salt

½ cup honey

½ teaspoon pure vanilla extract

1 cup plain nonfat yogurt

2 large eggs

1. Preheat oven to 375°F. Line a 24-cup mini muffin pan with paper liners.

2. In a large bowl, mix together flours, cornmeal, baking soda, and salt.

3. Add honey, vanilla, yogurt, and eggs to the bowl and mix with a rubber spatula until well blended, about 1 minute. You don't want to overmix or the muffins may be tough; just a thorough stir will do.

4. Use a small ice cream scoop or a tablespoon to scoop batter into the prepared mini muffin pan; the batter should fill about ¾ of each cup.

5. Bake 10–12 minutes or until a toothpick inserted in the center of a muffin comes out clean.

6. Let the muffins cool in the pan before serving.

Calories: 80 | Fat: 2g | Protein: 3g | Sodium: 160mg | Fiber: 0g | Carbohydrates: 14g | Sugar: 6g | Added Sugar: 5g

¼ cup plus ½ teaspoon canola oil, divided

1 cup whole-wheat flour

¾ cup unsweetened cocoa powder

¾ teaspoon baking soda

¼ teaspoon baking powder

½ teaspoon salt

2 large eggs

¼ cup plain low-fat Greek yogurt

¼ cup granulated sugar

¼ cup agave syrup

1 teaspoon pure vanilla extract

1½ cups shredded zucchini (about 2 medium zucchini), drained well

CHOCOLATE ZUCCHINI BREAD

This Chocolate Zucchini Bread is rich and moist and flavored with unsweetened cocoa powder for that chocolate intensity that kids (and adults) crave. But you can feel good knowing that each slice has 3 grams of fiber, providing more than 10 percent of the daily value of this often underconsumed nutrient.

1. Preheat oven to 350°F. Grease a 9" × 5" loaf pan with ½ teaspoon canola oil.

2. In a large bowl, stir together flour, cocoa powder, baking soda, baking powder, and salt. Set aside.

3. In a separate large bowl, whisk together eggs, remaining oil, yogurt, sugar, agave, and vanilla.

4. Add the flour mixture to the egg mixture. Stir to combine, about 2 minutes.

5. Fold in zucchini using a spatula. Pour into the prepared loaf pan.

6. Bake 50–55 minutes or until a toothpick inserted in the center comes out clean.

7. Let cool 10 minutes before removing from the pan. Use a bread knife to cut into 12 slices. Serve warm.

Calories: 140 | Fat: 7g | Protein: 4g | Sodium: 190mg | Fiber: 3g | Carbohydrates: 20g | Sugar: 9g | Added Sugar: 9g

½ teaspoon canola oil

⅓ cup granulated sugar

⅓ cup honey

½ cup unsalted butter, softened

2 large eggs

2 cups all-purpose flour

1½ teaspoons baking soda

½ teaspoon salt

1 teaspoon ground cinnamon

½ teaspoon ground nutmeg

¼ teaspoon ground ginger

1 cup pumpkin purée

PUMPKIN BREAD

This hearty and moist Pumpkin Bread is spiced with traditional pumpkin pie spices, making it perfect for breakfast or snacks. For a flavor twist you can substitute the puréed pumpkin with puréed sweet potatoes and still get amazing results. This bread freezes well up to 1 month, so make a double batch and enjoy one now and freeze the other for later.

1. Preheat oven to 350°F. Grease a 9" × 5" loaf pan with ½ teaspoon canola oil.

2. In a stand mixer with the paddle attachment, combine sugar, honey, and butter on low speed until smooth, about 2 minutes, scraping down the bowl with a spatula several times to make sure all ingredients are well mixed.

3. Add eggs; mix 1 minute, again scraping down bowl as needed.

4. Add flour, baking soda, salt, cinnamon, nutmeg, and ginger all at once and turn the mixer on slowly. Scrape down bowl again; make sure to get all the butter off the sides of the bowl and into the batter.

5. Add pumpkin purée; mix on low until batter has come together, about 2 minutes.

6. Pour batter into the prepared pan and bake 50–60 minutes or until a toothpick inserted in the center comes out clean.

7. Allow bread to cool in pan at least 20 minutes. Seal in plastic wrap or a zip-top bag when cooled and keep at room temperature up to 1 week.

Calories: 210 | Fat: 9g | Protein: 3g | Sodium: 270mg | Fiber: 1g | Carbohydrates: 30g | Sugar: 12g | Added Sugar: 11g

Chapter 6

DINNER

As tempting as it may be to order a carry-out meal for dinner, there are many benefits to making a home-cooked meal. Home-cooked meals tend to be lower in calories, sugar, and fat than their restaurant counterparts. Families who regularly eat home-cooked meals typically have better overall nutrient intake, healthier body weights, and higher intakes of fruits and vegetables compared to families who eat more restaurant meals.

The good news is, getting a home-cooked dinner on the table doesn't need to be a complicated ordeal. After all, there's already enough stress at the end of the day without making things more difficult than they need to be.

The recipes in this chapter are designed to help you put wholesome, healthy meals on the table in as little time as possible. You'll see that many of the recipes require just 10 minutes or less of hands-on time, freeing you up to spend time with your family rather than slaving over the stove. The recipes emphasize a plant-based approach to eating, featuring lots of fruits, vegetables, nuts, and grains, with small amounts of high-quality protein. They also use cooking methods that help bring out the natural sweetness of foods to help satiate your family's sweet cravings without all the sugar. A simpler, healthier dinnertime awaits you.

Serves 8
(serving size: 1 pizza bomb)

PREP: 20 minutes
COOK: 10 minutes

EASY PIZZA DOUGH

2 cups lukewarm water

½ (0.25-ounce) packet active dry yeast

1 teaspoon honey

1 tablespoon plus 1 teaspoon olive oil

1 teaspoon salt

2 cups plus 2 tablespoons all-purpose flour, divided

1 cup white whole-wheat flour

POPEYE PIZZA BOMBS

These little balls of baked pizza dough are stuffed with a luscious combination of tomato sauce, gooey cheese, and Popeye's favorite food, spinach. This recipe gives you the instructions to make your own simple pizza dough, but for a faster version, feel free to use 1 pound of store-bought pizza dough. And, because everyone loves to dip, serve these pizza bombs with a side of homemade Marinara Sauce (see Chapter 9).

1. First make the dough: Pour water into large mixing bowl; add yeast, honey, 1 tablespoon olive oil, and salt.

2. Add 2 cups all-purpose flour and 1 cup whole-wheat flour to water mixture and knead with your hands or mixer until it's smooth and elastic, about 10 minutes.

3. Lightly grease a medium bowl with remaining olive oil. Place dough in bowl, cover with plastic wrap, and let rise in a dry, warm area 2 hours.

4. Gently deflate dough and divide into 8 equal pieces, each about 2" in diameter. (Note: if using dough to make the Grilled Margarita Pizza recipe in this chapter, divide dough into 2 equal pieces.)

5. Sprinkle 2 tablespoons all-purpose flour onto work surface. Roll each piece of dough with a floured rolling pin into a 4" circle. Let dough rest several times in between rolling to allow it to relax so it is easier to handle. Turn dough over between rests to roll reverse side.

6. Preheat oven to 450°F. Line a baking sheet with parchment paper.

7. **To make the pizza bombs:** In a small skillet over medium heat, warm olive oil. Add garlic and oregano; stir 2–3 minutes until garlic begins to soften. Remove from heat; add salt and parsley. Set aside herb oil.

8. Spread ¼ teaspoon tomato paste in the center of each 4" circle of dough. Top with ⅛ cup spinach, followed by ⅛ cup mozzarella.

9. Use a pastry brush to lightly brush the circumference of the dough circles with water. Bring the edges of each dough circle together toward the center and pinch to seal. Use a metal skewer coated in flour to poke a hole in the top center of each pizza bomb to create a steam vent. Transfer to the prepared baking sheet.

10. Use a pastry brush to coat the top of each pizza bomb with equal amounts of the prepared herb oil. Bake 10 minutes. Serve warm.

....

Calories: 290 | Fat: 10g | Protein: 9g | Sodium: 640mg | Fiber: 3g | Carbohydrates: 42g | Sugar: 4g | Added Sugar: 1g

PIZZA BOMBS

2 tablespoons olive oil

1 clove garlic, minced

1 teaspoon dried oregano

¼ teaspoon salt

1 tablespoon finely chopped fresh flat-leaf Italian parsley

2 teaspoons unsalted tomato paste

1 cup roughly chopped baby spinach

1 cup shredded part-skim mozzarella

2 teaspoons water

1 pound pizza dough

1 tablespoon all-purpose flour

4 tablespoons olive oil, divided

8 ounces fresh mozzarella cheese, sliced ¼" thick

2 large ripe tomatoes, stemmed and thinly sliced

½ cup loosely packed basil leaves, cut into a chiffonade (thin strips)

½ teaspoon garlic powder

¼ teaspoon flaky sea salt

GRILLED MARGARITA PIZZA

Grilling pizza is a tasty alternative to oven-baked pizza, especially in the summer. The result is a light, crispy crust that pairs perfectly with the ingredients of a traditional margarita pizza: fresh summer tomatoes and basil. You can make your own simple pizza dough from scratch using the instructions for the Easy Pizza Dough in the Popeye Pizza Bombs recipe in this chapter, or to save time, use 1 pound of store-bought pizza dough.

1. If using store-bought pizza dough, allow dough to reach room temperature, about 1 hour. If using homemade dough, follow dough instructions in the Popeye Pizza Bombs recipe in this chapter.

2. Preheat outdoor grill to medium heat. Make sure grill grate is scrubbed clean.

3. Place two 14" pieces of parchment paper on a work surface. Divide dough evenly in half, placing 1 ball of dough onto each piece of parchment paper.

4. Lightly flour a rolling pin with the flour and roll out each half of dough into a 12" circle. Let dough rest several times in between rolling to allow it to relax so it is easier to handle. Turn dough over between rests to roll reverse side.

5. Use a pastry brush to spread 1 tablespoon olive oil on top of each dough circle.

6. Use a wooden pizza peel or baking sheet to carry pizza dough out to grill. Be sure to have all remaining ingredients prepared and set at a workstation next to grill.

7. Carefully flip the dough off the parchment paper onto the grill, oiled side down. Close grill cover and grill 3–5 minutes until dough is set with grill marks.

8. Use tongs to flip dough and then, moving very quickly and carefully, use a pastry brush to spread on remaining olive oil (1 tablespoon per pizza), then sprinkle on cheese, tomatoes, basil, garlic powder, and salt, dividing evenly between the pizzas. Close lid and grill 5–8 minutes or until cheese is melted and bottom of pizza is set with grill marks.

9. Use tongs to transfer pizzas from grill back to the pizza peel or baking sheet. Let stand 5 minutes, then slice and serve.

....

Calories: 340 | Fat: 16g | Protein: 11g | Sodium: 450mg | Fiber: 3g | Carbohydrates: 38g | Sugar: 2g | Added Sugar: 1g

VEGGIE LASAGNA CUPS

Serves 12
(serving size: 2 lasagna cups)

PREP: 10 minutes
COOK: 20 minutes

These cute little lasagna cups, filled with fresh zucchini and two kinds of cheese, are a perfectly portioned meal that kids love to eat with their hands (so make sure you have plenty of napkins on hand!). Serve them with a simple side salad and warm whole-wheat dinner rolls to round out the meal. Freeze any leftovers in an airtight container up to 1 month.

1. Preheat oven to 350°F. Spray 2 (12-cup) muffin tins with cooking spray.

2. Crack egg into a medium bowl; whisk. Add ricotta, Parmesan, oregano, salt, and pepper. Mix until well combined, about 1 minute.

3. Put a wonton wrapper into each cup of the muffin pans. Push center down so wrapper forms a cup. Scoop 1 tablespoon ricotta mixture into each wonton cup. Place 1 zucchini round in each cup on top of ricotta mixture and gently press down. Add 1 tablespoon marinara sauce to each wonton cup to cover zucchini rounds, then top each with 1 tablespoon mozzarella.

4. Bake 20 minutes or until edges of wontons are golden brown and crisp.

5. Let cups cool slightly, about 5 minutes. Remove and top with basil before serving.

Cooking spray

1 large egg

1¼ cups part-skim ricotta cheese

2 tablespoons grated Parmesan cheese

1 teaspoon dried oregano

½ teaspoon salt

¼ teaspoon freshly ground black pepper

24 wonton wrappers

2 medium zucchini, sliced into 24 (⅛"-thick) rounds

1½ cup Marinara Sauce, divided (see Chapter 9)

1½ cups shredded mozzarella cheese, divided

¼ cup thinly sliced fresh basil leaves

Calories: 150 | Fat: 5g | Protein: 9g | Sodium: 610mg | Fiber: 0g | Carbohydrates: 15g | Sugar: 3g | Added Sugar: 0g

ORECCHIETTE WITH ROASTED BROCCOLI, TOMATOES, AND WALNUTS

12 ounces orecchiette

2 tablespoons unsalted butter

2 medium heads broccoli, cut into small florets

½ cup halved cherry tomatoes

½ cup chopped walnuts

¼ cup olive oil

2 cloves garlic, chopped

½ teaspoon kosher salt

½ teaspoon freshly ground black pepper

¼ cup grated Parmesan cheese

¼ cup thinly sliced fresh basil leaves

This recipe, or some variation of it, is in regular rotation in my home. The following combination is one of our favorites, but I'll often swap in other veggies and sometimes add chicken sausage. Sometimes I'll even serve it "deconstructed" so that everyone can pick which ingredients they want in their pasta bowl. If you don't have orecchiette, you can substitute with another pasta shape, such as penne or bowtie.

1. Preheat oven to 400°F.

2. Cook orecchiette according to package directions, about 10 minutes. Reserve ¾ cup of the cooking water, drain the pasta, and return it to the pot. Immediately add the reserved water and butter; toss to coat.

3. Meanwhile, toss broccoli, tomatoes, walnuts, olive oil, garlic, salt, and pepper to a rimmed baking sheet. Roast 20 minutes, tossing halfway through.

4. Toss broccoli mixture into the pasta. Transfer to a medium serving bowl and sprinkle with Parmesan and basil. Serve immediately.

Calories: 410 | Fat: 21g | Protein: 11g | Sodium: 270mg | Fiber: 2g | Carbohydrates: 46g | Sugar: 3g | Added Sugar: 0g

SWEET POTATO NOODLE CARBONARA

Serves 4

PREP: 10 minutes
COOK: 15 minutes

This twist on a traditional pasta carbonara is an easy, nutrient-rich favorite. You can spiralize your own sweet potatoes using a vegetable spiralizer, or most supermarkets now carry pre-spiralized sweet potatoes, helping you save time. Another tasty variation is to make this recipe with spiralized zucchini. For an added protein boost, top each serving with a simple fried egg.

6 strips low-sodium turkey bacon

1 tablespoon olive oil

6 cups sweet potato noodles

2 cloves garlic, minced

½ teaspoon salt

¼ teaspoon freshly ground black pepper

½ cup grated Parmesan cheese

½ cup chopped fresh flat-leaf Italian parsley

1. Place turkey bacon in a single layer in a large unheated skillet. Heat 7–9 minutes or to desired crispiness over medium heat, turning several times. Remove from skillet and set aside.

2. Add olive oil to skillet and add sweet potato noodles, garlic, salt, and pepper. Toss sweet potato noodles lightly with tongs and cook about 5 minutes.

3. Crumble or cut turkey bacon. Add to sweet potato noodles and toss.

4. Remove from heat. Place in medium serving bowl. Sprinkle with Parmesan and parsley before serving.

Calories: 390 | Fat: 11g | Protein: 11g | Sodium: 840mg | Fiber: 9g | Carbohydrates: 64g | Sugar: 13g | Added Sugar: 0g

Serves 12

PREP: 15 minutes
COOK: 10 minutes

SIMPLE BBQ CHICKEN SLIDERS

1 (4-pound) organic rotisserie chicken, skin removed, shredded

1½ cup Sweet and Tangy Barbecue Sauce (see Chapter 9)

12 whole-grain slider buns

12 leaves Boston lettuce

1 cup shredded purple cabbage

½ cup peeled and shredded carrots

These Simple BBQ Chicken Sliders are made with shredded rotisserie chicken for a major time-saver. I've made this for many get-togethers and, every time, people ooh and aah, asking if I smoked a chicken all day. Nope! Serve this dish with an assortment of veggie-rich salads, such as Lemon Broccoli (Chapter 7), Oil and Vinegar Coleslaw (Chapter 7), Grilled Corn Salad (Chapter 7), and Grilled Kale Chips (Chapter 7).

Toss shredded chicken with barbecue sauce in a small soup pot and heat on medium heat 5–10 minutes, until sauce begins to simmer. Evenly distribute between slider buns. Top each with even amounts of lettuce, cabbage, and carrots. Serve warm.

Calories: 120 | Fat: 3g | Protein: 14g | Sodium: 280mg | Fiber: 1g | Carbohydrates: 10g | Sugar: 7g | Added Sugar: 5g

3 tablespoons coconut oil

2 cups whole-wheat panko

½ teaspoon garlic powder

½ teaspoon salt

¼ teaspoon freshly ground black pepper

1 large egg, beaten

2 tablespoons skim milk

¾ cup whole-wheat flour

1 pound boneless, skinless chicken breasts, cut into bite-sized pieces

Cooking spray

CRISPY CHICKEN NUGGETS

This is the kind of recipe that you make for the kids, but all the adults end up devouring. These crunchy, juicy little nuggets are coated in whole-grain panko and then baked, for a much healthier take than what you might buy in a drive-through. Serve with a veggie side and Homemade Ketchup (see Chapter 9), Honey Mustard Dip (see Chapter 9), or Quick Ranch Dip (see Chapter 9).

1. Preheat oven to 425°F. Place a wire rack inside a baking sheet.

2. Melt coconut oil in a small skillet over low heat. Add panko, garlic powder, salt, and pepper and slowly stir until golden brown, about 5 minutes.

3. Put three shallow dishes on a work surface. Fill one with egg and milk (whisked together), the second with flour, and the third with the panko mixture.

4. Dunk chicken into egg mixture, then flour, and shake off excess. Dunk chicken in egg mixture again and then roll in panko, coating thoroughly. Use your fingers to press bread crumbs into chicken. Place chicken pieces on the wire rack in baking pan.

5. Once all chicken pieces are breaded and on rack, spray top of the nuggets with cooking spray. Bake 10 minutes or until chicken is fully cooked (internal temperature of 165°F). Let rest 5 minutes before serving.

Calories: 300 | Fat: 10g | Protein: 25g | Sodium: 290mg | Fiber: 2g | Carbohydrates: 30g | Sugar: 1g | Added Sugar: 0g

PROTEIN-PACKED TURKEY MEATBALLS

Serves 6

PREP: 10 minutes
COOK: 25 minutes

These tasty turkey meatballs are spiked with fresh mint and coarsely grated zucchini, which helps keep them moist. Another special ingredient is hemp hearts, which helps boost the protein content. The flavor profile of these meatballs pairs perfectly with warm pita, Classic Hummus (see Chapter 9), Herby Tahini Dip (see Chapter 9), and Honey-Roasted Carrots (see Chapter 7).

1. Preheat oven to 450°F. Drizzle olive oil into an 8" × 8" baking dish; use your hands to coat the entire dish evenly.

2. In a large mixing bowl, combine all remaining ingredients. Mix with a fork or by hand until ingredients are thoroughly incorporated.

3. Roll mixture into round 1" meatballs, packing the meat together firmly. Place balls in the prepared baking dish, lining them up snugly in even rows so the meatballs touch each other.

4. Roast 20–25 minutes or until cooked through (a meat thermometer inserted into the center of a meatball should read 165°F). Once cooked, allow meatballs to cool in baking dish 5 minutes. Transfer to a medium bowl or platter and serve.

Calories: 160 | Fat: 7g | Protein: 22g | Sodium: 260mg | Fiber: 1g | Carbohydrates: 3g | Sugar: 1g | Added Sugar: 0g

1 tablespoon olive oil

1 pound ground turkey breast

1 medium zucchini, coarsely grated

2 green onions, thinly sliced

2 tablespoons chopped fresh mint

1 large egg

¼ cup shelled hemp hearts

1 clove garlic, minced

½ teaspoon salt

¼ teaspoon freshly ground black pepper

Hemp Hearts

Hemp hearts are hemp seeds from which the hard outer shell has been removed. Hemp hearts are rich in protein and have all ten essential amino acids. They also contain omega-3 and omega-6 fatty acids, including gamma-linolenic acid (GLA), which has been to shown to help with cholesterol, inflammation, skin and hair health, and overall heart health.

HOMEMADE MACARONI AND CHEESE

16 cups water

1 cup whole-wheat panko

1 tablespoon unsalted butter, melted

1 pound whole-grain elbow macaroni

1 tablespoon salt

3 (12-ounce) cans low-fat 2% evaporated milk

½ teaspoon dry mustard

½ teaspoon garlic powder

½ teaspoon freshly ground black pepper

1 tablespoon cornstarch

2 cups shredded reduced-fat Cheddar cheese

When it comes to comfort foods, nothing quite beats mac and cheese. But most homemade versions are loaded with calories and fat, while boxed versions lack the flavor and texture that makes the dish so crave-worthy. This recipe uses low-fat evaporated milk and reduced-fat Cheddar to rein in the fat, while still delivering on flavor. And like most mac and cheeses, there's no sugar added.

1. Preheat oven to 350°F.

2. Bring water to boil in a large pot.

3. While water is reaching a boil, toast panko in a large, dry skillet over medium heat until well-browned, about 5–10 minutes, stirring often. Transfer to a medium mixing bowl; pour melted butter over panko and stir to combine. Set aside.

4. Once water reaches a boil, add macaroni and salt. Stir macaroni every 2–3 minutes and cook until al dente, about 8 minutes. Reserve ¼ cup cooking water, then drain macaroni.

5. In the pot, combine milk, mustard, garlic, and pepper. Bring to simmer over medium heat.

6. Meanwhile, in a small mixing bowl, whisk together cornstarch and reserved pasta water until smooth. Whisk into simmering pot. Continue to whisk constantly while simmering until sauce begins to thicken, about 3 minutes.

7. Remove from heat. Whisk in Cheddar in small batches until fully melted. Stir in cooked macaroni.

8. Transfer macaroni and cheese to a 13" × 9" baking dish. Sprinkle panko mixture over top. Bake 20 minutes on middle rack of oven. Let cool slightly before serving.

Calories: 300 | Fat: 7g | Protein: 19g | Sodium: 250mg | Fiber: 0g | Carbohydrates: 45g | Sugar: 10g | Added Sugar: 0g

SAUSAGE AND PEPPERS SHEET PAN

Serves 4

PREP: **10 minutes**
COOK: **30 minutes**

This all-in-one dish is a snap to whip together. Best of all, there's only one pan to clean! I like to use precooked chicken sausage, but any type will do. Important note: if you use raw sausage, leave the links whole and add them to the baking sheet with the onions, so they can cook for the full length of the recipe (about 25 minutes), then let cool slightly and slice. Serve with Smashed Potato Bites (see Chapter 7), whole-grain hoagies, and spicy mustard.

1 small yellow onion, top removed, halved, peeled, and thinly sliced

2 tablespoons olive oil, divided

1 teaspoon Italian seasoning, divided

½ teaspoon freshly ground black pepper, divided

1 medium green bell pepper, stemmed, seeded, and thinly sliced

1 medium red bell pepper, stemmed, seeded, and thinly sliced

1 medium yellow bell pepper, stemmed, seeded, and thinly sliced

1 (12-ounce) package Italian sausage, fully cooked, sliced into ½" rounds

1. Preheat oven to 425°F. Line a rimmed baking sheet with parchment paper.

2. Spread onion evenly on baking sheet. Drizzle with 1 tablespoon olive oil; sprinkle with ½ teaspoon Italian seasoning and ¼ teaspoon black pepper. Use a spatula to gently toss. Roast 5 minutes.

3. Use a spatula to move onions to one side of baking sheet. Spread bell peppers evenly on baking sheet. Drizzle with 1 tablespoon olive oil; sprinkle with ½ teaspoon Italian seasoning and ¼ teaspoon black pepper. Use a spatula to gently toss. Roast 15 minutes, separately stirring peppers and onions halfway through.

4. Use a spatula to group bell peppers to middle of baking sheet. Add Italian sausage slices to empty ⅓ of sheet. Return to oven and bake 8–10 minutes until onions and peppers are slightly charred and sausage is thoroughly warmed.

Calories: 220 | Fat: 14g | Protein: 15g | Sodium: 490mg | Fiber: 2g | Carbohydrates: 10g | Sugar: 3g | Added Sugar: 0g

BLACK BEAN AND AVOCADO TACOS

Serves 4
(serving size: 2 tacos)

PREP: 10 minutes
COOK: 10 minutes

Not that anyone ever needs an excuse to eat tacos (every day, please!), but Taco Tuesday has officially put it into regular rotation in my kitchen. When it comes to tortillas, corn tortillas are definitely the way to go. Most flour tortillas have a long ingredient list filled with preservatives and even added sugar. Corn tortillas, on the other hand, generally have no added sugar and are naturally higher in fiber.

1 tablespoon olive oil

1 clove garlic, minced

1 (15-ounce) can low-sodium black beans (undrained)

1 teaspoon ground cumin

1 teaspoon ground coriander

1 teaspoon garlic powder

½ teaspoon chili powder

8 (6") corn tortillas

2 medium avocados, pitted, peeled, and each sliced into 8 strips

8 ounces Cotija cheese

¼ cup minced red onion

½ cup chopped fresh cilantro

2 large limes, cut into 4 wedges each

1. Place a medium skillet over medium-low heat. Add olive oil and minced garlic. Cook 2 minutes until garlic begins to soften. Add beans, cumin, coriander, garlic powder, and chili powder. Continue to heat, stirring occasionally, until most liquid has been absorbed, about 5 minutes. Remove from heat; transfer beans to a medium serving bowl.

2. Lightly toast tortillas on gas burner. Alternatively, place 4 tortillas at a time on a plate, cover with a tea towel, and microwave in 30-second bursts on high until warmed through. Wrap in a tea towel to keep warm.

3. Lay out 2 tortillas on each serving plate. Top each tortilla with equal amounts black bean mixture, avocado strips, cheese, onion, and cilantro. Serve with lime wedges.

Calories: 580 | Fat: 33g | Protein: 23g | Sodium: 950mg | Fiber: 13g | Carbohydrates: 53g | Sugar: 1g | Added Sugar: 0g

Cooking spray

2 cups shredded cooked chicken

½ teaspoon chili powder

¼ teaspoon paprika

¼ teaspoon ground cumin

¼ teaspoon garlic powder

¼ teaspoon onion powder

¼ teaspoon salt

¼ teaspoon freshly ground black pepper

1 tablespoon fresh lime juice

1 cup shredded reduced-fat Mexican cheese blend

24 (6") corn tortillas

BAKED CHICKEN TAQUITOS

Taquitos are basically tacos that have been rolled up and fried. This recipe deviates from the traditional preparation style by baking them, but trust me, you'll still get perfectly golden and crunchy taquitos. When you're ready to serve them, create a toppings bar with lettuce, diced tomato, sliced green onions, guacamole, and sour cream so everyone can top them to their heart's content.

1. Preheat oven to 425°F. Coat a baking sheet with cooking spray.

2. In a medium bowl, combine chicken, chili powder, paprika, cumin, garlic powder, onion powder, salt, pepper, and lime juice. Stir until ingredients are well combined. Add shredded cheese and stir again.

3. Soften tortillas by placing 12 between two wet paper towels and microwaving 30 seconds, then repeating with remaining tortillas.

4. Working with 1 tortilla at a time, place 2 tablespoons chicken mixture on the bottom half of the tortilla, then tightly roll it up and place it on the prepared baking sheet, seam side down. Repeat with remaining ingredients.

5. Spray taquitos liberally with cooking spray and bake until crispy, about 15 minutes. Serve warm.

Calories: 180 | Fat: 4g | Protein: 13g | Sodium: 140mg | Fiber: 0g | Carbohydrates: 25g | Sugar: 0g | Added Sugar: 0g

10-MINUTE VEGGIE FRIED RICE

Serves 8

PREP: 5 minutes
COOK: 10 minutes

I love anything quick and easy, so this recipe is especially high on my go-to list. Most of the ingredients are things you can easily have on stock in your pantry and freezer, making it a great option for when you need to have dinner on the table in 10 minutes but don't have a plan. Feel free to add a protein option, like chicken, shrimp, or tofu.

1 tablespoon canola oil

2 cups frozen peas and carrots

½ cup raw unsalted whole cashews

1 (8-ounce) can pineapple chunks (in 100% juice), drained

1 teaspoon salt

1½ teaspoons ground ginger

1 teaspoon garlic powder

2 large eggs

6 cups cooked brown rice

½ cup low-sodium soy sauce

½ cup diced green onion

1. Warm oil in a large pan over medium heat. Add peas and carrots; stir 1 minute. Add cashews and pineapple. Top with salt, ginger, and garlic powder; continue to sauté about 5 minutes.

2. Push mixture to side of pan; drop in eggs and scramble until cooked, about 2 minutes.

3. Add rice and soy sauce; sauté 1 minute. Remove from heat. Top with green onion and serve.

Calories: 330 | Fat: 9g | Protein: 10g | Sodium: 730mg | Fiber: 9g | Carbohydrates: 56g | Sugar: 7g | Added Sugar: 0g

SPICY PEANUT NOODLES WITH SHRIMP

This protein-packed noodle dish comes together in 15 minutes flat, speedier than a delivery order could be at your door. While this dish has a tiny bit of kick, it's totally manageable, even for delicate palates. If shrimp isn't your thing, replace it with another protein of your choice, such as chicken or tofu. Serve with lime wedges on the side for a little citrus zing.

1 teaspoon canola oil

2 teaspoons minced fresh ginger

2 cloves garlic, minced

1 tablespoon low-sodium soy sauce

1 tablespoon rice vinegar

½ teaspoon sriracha sauce

⅓ cup natural creamy peanut butter

½ cup low-sodium vegetable broth

4 cups cold water

2 teaspoons salt

8 ounces whole-grain spaghetti

12 ounces medium shrimp, peeled and deveined

1 medium red bell pepper, seeded and cut into thin strips

1 cup snow peas, cut into thin strips

1 large carrot, peeled and cut into thin strips about 3" long

¼ cup coarsely chopped unsalted peanuts

¼ cup roughly chopped cilantro

1 medium lime, cut into 4 wedges (optional)

1. Add oil, ginger, and garlic to a medium skillet and heat on medium 2 minutes, stirring continuously. Add soy sauce, vinegar, sriracha, peanut butter, and broth. Continue stirring until peanut butter melts, 2–3 minutes. Reduce heat to low and simmer 8 minutes until the sauce begins to thicken.

2. Meanwhile, add water to a large pot; stir in salt and bring to a boil. Cook spaghetti 6 minutes. Add shrimp to the pot and cook 5 minutes. Add bell pepper, snow peas, and carrot to the pot; cook 1 minute. Drain.

3. Return spaghetti, shrimp, and vegetables to pot. Add peanut sauce and toss until well combined. Transfer to large serving bowl. Top with peanuts and cilantro. Serve warm with optional lime wedges on the side.

Calories: 300 | Fat: 17g | Protein: 20g | Sodium: 700mg | Fiber: 4g | Carbohydrates: 14g | Sugar: 5g | Added Sugar: 0g

ROASTED RED PEPPER AND TOMATO SOUP

2 large red bell peppers

1 tablespoon olive oil

½ medium yellow onion, peeled and roughly chopped

1 large carrot, peeled and roughly chopped

1 (28-ounce) can unsalted diced tomatoes

4 sun-dried tomatoes

1 (13.5-ounce) can light coconut milk

2 teaspoons garlic powder

2 teaspoons herbes de Provence

½ teaspoon sea salt

½ teaspoon freshly ground black pepper

This soup is similar to classic tomato soup, but it's made sweeter with the addition of roasted red bell pepper and light coconut milk. It's great for a light stand-alone meal and also makes a perfect partner to a grilled cheese sandwich. The soup holds up well in the refrigerator up to 5 days and freezes up to 1 month.

1. Preheat oven to 500°F. Line a baking sheet with foil. Place whole red bell peppers on sheet and roast about 15 minutes, flipping several times to evenly char all sides.

2. When peppers are charred, remove from oven and cover with an upside-down bowl 10 minutes to "steam" the peppers. This will help loosen the skin. Once peppers are cool, peel off skin, slice peppers in half, and remove stem and seeds. Then roughly chop.

3. Heat olive oil in a large pot over medium heat. Add onion and carrot and cook about 5 minutes until onions soften, stirring occasionally. Add roasted peppers and all remaining ingredients, stirring to combine. Reduce heat to medium-low and simmer 15 minutes.

4. Turn off heat and use an immersion blender to purée soup until smooth, about 2–3 minutes. Turn heat back on to medium-low and continue to simmer an additional 15 minutes to allow the flavors to meld.

Calories: 130 | Fat: 6g | Protein: 2g | Sodium: 240mg | Fiber: 3g | Carbohydrates: 16g | Sugar: 9g | Added Sugar: 0g

ALPHABET MINESTRONE SOUP

Serves 8

PREP: 10 minutes
COOK: 40 minutes

This veggie-packed minestrone is made kid-friendly by using alphabet noodles in lieu of traditional noodle shapes. If you can't find them at your local grocery store, you can find them at most major online grocery retailers. The addition of pesto adds all the flavor of fresh herbs with less prep work. This nutrient-rich soup is a perfect dish to serve on any cold day, and especially when you may need to balance out an otherwise indulgent day.

1. In a large stockpot over medium heat, warm olive oil and sauté onion until soft, about 5 minutes. Add leeks and garlic; sauté 2–3 minutes, stirring frequently to prevent any browning. Add carrots, celery, and tomatoes; cook 2–3 minutes, stirring frequently.

2. Add broth and black pepper; increase heat and bring to a boil. Once boiling, reduce heat to medium-low and simmer 20 minutes.

3. Add zucchini, noodles, and beans. Return to a boil 8–10 minutes or until the noodles are al dente. Remove from heat and let cool 5 minutes. Stir in pesto and Parmesan cheese, then serve.

Calories: 230 | Fat: 10g | Protein: 8g | Sodium: 390mg | Fiber: 5g | Carbohydrates: 27g | Sugar: 6g | Added Sugar: 0g

1 tablespoon olive oil

1 small yellow onion, peeled and diced

1 leek, greens removed, whites quartered and sliced

2 cloves garlic, minced

2 large carrots, peeled and sliced into thin rounds

2 stalks celery, cut into ¼" dice

2 large ripe tomatoes, stems removed, cut into ½" dice

6 cups low-sodium vegetable broth

½ teaspoon freshly ground black pepper

1 medium zucchini, quartered and diced

½ cup alphabet noodles

1 (15-ounce) can unsalted navy beans, drained and rinsed

½ cup pesto

½ cup freshly grated Parmesan cheese

SMOKY LENTIL SOUP

1 tablespoon olive oil

1 small yellow onion, peeled and diced

1 clove garlic, minced

2 large carrots, peeled and cut into ¼" dice

1 stalk celery, cut into ¼" dice

1 tablespoon unsalted tomato paste

1 teaspoon smoked paprika

1 large tomato, stemmed and diced

¾ cup dried red lentils, picked over and rinsed

4 cups low-sodium chicken broth

½ teaspoon freshly ground black pepper

This puréed soup is a great way to stealthily increase your family's intake of lentils. Feel free to purée it to your desired consistency. I purée it halfway so that some texture from the lentils remains. But for pickier eaters, a smoother consistency is best. If desired, garnish with sour cream or bacon bits. To round out the meal, serve with a simple green salad or an Apple Cheddar Melt (see Chapter 4).

1. In a large stockpot over medium heat, warm olive oil. Add onion and sauté until soft, about 5 minutes. Add garlic and sauté another 2 minutes, stirring frequently to prevent any browning. Add carrots, celery, tomato paste, and paprika; cook 2–3 minutes, stirring frequently.

2. Add tomatoes, lentils, and broth; stir. Increase heat and bring to a boil. Once boiling, reduce heat to maintain a low simmer, cover, and continue to cook until lentils are tender, about 35–40 minutes.

3. Turn heat off and use an immersion blender to purée soup to desired consistency. Season with black pepper and garnish as desired.

Calories: 160 | Fat: 4g | Protein: 11g | Sodium: 75mg | Fiber: 5g | Carbohydrates: 22g | Sugar: 4g | Added Sugar: 0g

Did You Know...?

A 100-gram serving of lentils offers the same amount of protein as found in a similar sized serving of steak, 72 percent of the daily recommended intake of fiber, and 25 percent of the daily recommended potassium intake, which is twice as much as a large banana!

VEGGIE CHILI

Serves 8

PREP: 15 minutes
COOK: 60 minutes

This three-bean chili is loaded with fresh vegetables for a much healthier take on a traditional chili. The addition of vegetarian burger crumbles gives it the texture that meat lovers will appreciate. Serve this hearty soup with a variety of garnishes such as shredded cheese, sour cream, scallions, and tortilla chips.

1. In a large stockpot over medium heat, warm olive oil. Add onion and sauté until soft, about 5 minutes. Add garlic and sauté another 2 minutes, stirring frequently to prevent any browning.

2. Add bell peppers, celery, jalapeño, chili powder, cumin, and oregano; cook 2–3 minutes, stirring frequently. Add burger crumbles and cook another 5 minutes, stirring occasionally.

3. Pour in tomatoes and beans. Add bay leaves. Bring to a boil, then reduce heat to low and simmer uncovered 45 minutes. Remove bay leaves and ladle into serving bowls.

Calories: 260 | Fat: 5g | Protein: 7g | Sodium: 260mg | Fiber: 11g | Carbohydrates: 38g | Sugar: 7g | Added Sugar: 0g

1 tablespoon olive oil

1 small yellow onion, peeled and diced

2 cloves garlic, minced

1 medium red bell pepper, seeded and chopped

1 medium green bell pepper, seeded and chopped

2 stalks celery, cut into ¼" dice

1 large jalapeño pepper, seeded and chopped

2 tablespoons chili powder

1 tablespoon ground cumin

2 tablespoons dried oregano

1 (12-ounce) package vegetarian burger crumbles

3 (14.5-ounce) cans unsalted diced tomatoes

1 (15-ounce) can unsalted kidney beans, drained

1 (15-ounce) can unsalted garbanzo beans, drained

1 (15-ounce) can unsalted black beans, drained

2 bay leaves

BUTTERNUT SQUASH SOUP

Serves 6

PREP: 20 minutes
COOK: 35 minutes

In the middle of the winter, when fresh produce is limited or imported from afar, hearty butternut squash adds a welcome pop of color and touch of natural sweetness to the menu. If you're looking to save time on meal prep, opt for precut butternut squash, although be forewarned that the color and texture doesn't match that of preparing one fresh. The crème fraîche and olive oil that are drizzled on at the end add just the right amount of creaminess to this dish, so don't be tempted to skip that step.

1 large butternut squash (about 3 pounds)

¼ cup unsalted butter

2 medium shallots, peeled and minced

6 cups low-sodium chicken broth

1 teaspoon minced fresh thyme

1 teaspoon minced fresh sage

½ teaspoon ground ginger

½ cup heavy cream

1 teaspoon dark brown sugar

¼ cup crème fraîche, divided

½ teaspoon sea salt

2 teaspoons freshly ground black pepper, divided

2 green onions, trimmed and sliced (white and green parts), divided

1 tablespoon extra-virgin olive oil, divided

1. Cut top and bottom off squash and use a vegetable peeler to remove skin. Cut squash in half lengthwise. Use a spoon to scoop out seeds and stringy fiber. Then cut each half into 4 pieces.

2. Heat butter in large stockpot over medium-low heat until it starts to bubble, about 3–5 minutes. Add shallots and stir about 10 minutes or until translucent.

3. Add broth, squash, thyme, sage, and ginger; bring to a boil over high heat. Reduce heat, cover, and simmer about 20 minutes or until squash is tender.

4. Transfer to a blender and purée squash in batches. Return soup to pot; stir in cream and brown sugar and bring to a low simmer until hot.

5. Ladle soup evenly into soup bowls. Top each with a dollop of crème fraîche, about 2 teaspoons per dollop. Sprinkle lightly with salt and grind black pepper over the top, about ⅓ teaspoon per bowl. Garnish with green onions, about 2 teaspoons per bowl. Drizzle ½ teaspoon olive oil over the top of each bowl and serve immediately.

Calories: 340 | Fat: 23g | Protein: 8g | Sodium: 290mg | Fiber: 5g | Carbohydrates: 32g | Sugar: 7g | Added Sugar: 1g

Shopping for Squash

When shopping for butternut squash, look for one with a vivid color and a dry, fibrous stem. Make sure the exterior feels hard without any soft spots. Then choose one that feels heavy for its size. This is a sign that the flesh is still moist and soft.

CRISPY FISH FINGERS

These flaky fish fingers are coated in a crispy batter made with whole-wheat panko and quinoa, then baked, resulting in a much lighter and healthier meal than the deep-fried kind. The quinoa is just slightly toasted, but otherwise remains un-cooked, giving it a crunch that amps up both the textural and nutritional variety of the recipe.

Cooking spray

½ cup uncooked white quinoa

1 cup whole-wheat panko

1 teaspoon lemon pepper seasoning

½ teaspoon paprika

½ teaspoon garlic powder

½ cup whole-wheat flour

2 large egg whites, beaten

1 pound skinless cod fillets, cut into 1" pieces

1. Preheat oven to 425°F. Line a baking sheet with parchment paper and lightly coat with cooking spray.

2. Heat quinoa in a large skillet over medium heat 3–5 minutes until lightly toasted, stirring occasionally. Remove from heat; let cool about 10 minutes.

3. Combine quinoa, panko, lemon pepper, paprika, and garlic powder in a food processor and pulse 30–60 seconds until finely ground. Transfer to a shallow dish.

4. Place flour in a second shallow dish and egg whites in a third shallow dish.

5. Dredge each piece of fish in flour, dip in egg, and then dredge in panko mixture, pressing to adhere. Place in the prepared pan. Lightly coat fish with cooking spray.

6. Bake until fish is cooked through and breading is golden and crisp, about 10 minutes. Serve warm.

Seafood Recommendations

The 2015–2020 Dietary Guidelines for Americans recommends that the general population should eat at least 8 ounces of seafood per week (4–5 ounces for young children) with the goal of getting at least 250 milligrams per day of the omega-3 fatty acids EPA (eicosapentaenoic acid) and DHA (docosahexaenoic acid).

Calories: 260 | Fat: 2.5g | Protein: 28g | Sodium: 110mg | Fiber: 2g | Carbohydrates: 32g | Sugar: 1g | Added Sugar: 0g

Chapter 7

SIDES

So often when it comes to planning meals, side dishes are an afterthought. As a result, many families don't eat enough vegetables, a food group that is jam-packed with disease-fighting, health-promoting nutrients.

Side dishes are a great way to improve the overall quality of your family's diet and give everyone more choices at the dinner table. You may even decide to make an entire balanced meal out of side dishes, which is a fresh and colorful way to feed your family.

The side dishes in this chapter are bursting with simple preparations of seasonal vegetables and other whole foods. While your kids may not be the biggest fan of vegetables yet, the kid-approved recipes in this chapter were developed to bring out and enhance the natural sweetness found in vegetables, helping to make them instant kid-favorites.

LEMON BROCCOLI

1 pound fresh broccoli

3 tablespoons olive oil, divided

1 tablespoon lemon juice

½ teaspoon sea salt

The Pros of Bitter

Cruciferous vegetables such as broccoli, cauliflower, cabbage, and kale all have a sulfur-containing compound called sulforaphane. Sulforaphane is what gives cruciferous vegetables their bitter taste, but also what gives them their cancer-fighting power. Blanching or roasting these vegetables and adding salt, spices, and/or acid (e.g., lemon juice) helps mask the bitter flavor while still allowing you to reap the health benefits cruciferous vegetables offer.

This roasted broccoli drizzled with fresh lemon juice and sprinkled with sea salt has turned my kids into bona fide broccoli lovers. In their minds, it's the one and only way to make broccoli. Bonus: it couldn't be easier to make. Serve it with whole-grain butter noodles and grilled chicken for a simple, satisfying meal.

1. Preheat oven to 425°F.

2. Cut the broccoli stem off, then slice the crown into medium-sized florets. Peel broccoli stem, then cut it into ½" pieces.

3. Drizzle a baking sheet with 1 tablespoon olive oil. In a large bowl, toss broccoli florets and stem pieces with remaining olive oil.

4. Spread broccoli on baking sheet and roast 20 minutes.

5. Use a spatula to flip the broccoli and roast 10 minutes or until it is as crisp as you like it.

6. Transfer broccoli to a medium serving bowl or platter. Drizzle with fresh lemon juice and sprinkle with salt. Enjoy immediately.

Calories: 80 | Fat: 7g | Protein: 2g | Sodium: 210mg | Fiber: 2g | Carbohydrates: 4g | Sugar: 2g | Added Sugar: 0g

CRISPY CAULIFLOWER

Serves 6

PREP: 10 minutes
COOK: 40 minutes

This is my family's favorite side dish, hands down. It's also one of the simplest to make. Roasting cauliflower brings out its natural sweetness, turning a bitter vegetable into something that kids will devour. I like to cut the cauliflower into tiny pieces and roast it for a full 40 minutes, so that it's extra crispy, but your family may prefer a slightly shorter cooking time.

1 pound fresh cauliflower

3 tablespoons olive oil, divided

½ teaspoon kosher salt

½ teaspoon freshly ground black pepper

1. Preheat oven to 425°F.

2. Cut cauliflower into tiny florets, the size of a quarter or smaller.

3. Drizzle a baking sheet with 1 tablespoon olive oil. In a large bowl, toss cauliflower with remaining olive oil, salt, and pepper.

4. Spread cauliflower on the baking sheet and roast 20 minutes.

5. Use a spatula to flip the cauliflower and roast 10–20 minutes or until it is as crisp as you like it.

6. Transfer cauliflower to a medium serving bowl or platter. Enjoy immediately.

Calories: 80 | Fat: 7g | Protein: 1g | Sodium: 180mg | Fiber: 2g | Carbohydrates: 4g | Sugar: 1g | Added Sugar: 0g

8 large carrots, peeled, quartered lengthwise, and cut into 3" pieces

4 tablespoons olive oil, divided

¼ teaspoon salt

3 tablespoons honey

½ cup warm water

¼ cup chopped toasted hazelnuts

HONEY-ROASTED CARROTS

Carrots are one of those vegetables that most kids like, thankfully. Whenever there's an ingredient that's widely accepted, I like to use it in new ways to help broaden the flavors and textures that kids will eat. These Honey-Roasted Carrots do the trick by pairing the carrots with sweet honey and crunchy hazelnuts.

1. Preheat oven to 450°F.

2. Toss the carrots with 3 tablespoons olive oil in a large bowl. Add salt and toss again.

3. In a small bowl, combine honey and warm water. Stir with a fork about 30 seconds until thoroughly combined.

4. Drizzle a large, rimmed baking sheet with remaining tablespoon olive oil. Transfer carrots to the baking sheet and use a fork or your fingers to spread them out evenly. Drizzle carrots evenly with honey mixture. Roast 25 minutes or until carrots are soft and golden brown around the edges.

5. Transfer carrots to a serving dish, sprinkle with hazelnuts, and serve warm.

Calories: 190 | Fat: 12g | Protein: 2g | Sodium: 150mg | Fiber: 3g | Carbohydrates: 23g | Sugar: 15g | Added Sugar: 9g

LEMONY SPRING SALAD

Serves 8

PREP: 10 minutes
COOK: N/A

One of our favorite Italian restaurants in Chicago serves a dish like this. It's simple, refreshing, and colorful. I like to prep everything in advance (up to a day before), then drizzle the dressing on immediately before serving. I often serve it as an appetizer when the kids are hungry but dinner's not quite ready.

1. Whisk together mustard, lemon juice, vinegar, and ½ teaspoon salt in a medium bowl. Slowly whisk in olive oil until smooth.

2. Add snap peas, cucumber, and tomatoes in a medium salad bowl. Drizzle dressing onto vegetables and toss to coat. Sprinkle with remaining salt.

1 tablespoon Dijon mustard

1 tablespoon fresh lemon juice

2 teaspoons red wine vinegar

1 teaspoon kosher salt, divided

3 tablespoons extra-virgin olive oil

2 cups sugar snap peas

1 medium cucumber, peeled and cut into ½" half-moons

1 pint cherry tomatoes

Calories: 70 | Fat: 5g | Protein: 1g | Sodium: 290mg | Fiber: 1g | Carbohydrates: 5g | Sugar: 3g | Added Sugar: 0g

1 pound carrots, peeled and
grated

¼ cup chopped fresh flat-leaf
Italian parsley

¼ cup raisins

3 tablespoons olive oil

2 teaspoons Dijon mustard

1 tablespoon lemon juice

1 teaspoon honey

½ teaspoon salt

½ teaspoon freshly ground black
pepper

CARROT AND RAISIN SALAD

I once made this dish with a class of kindergarteners. You may think that serving salad to a group of five-year-olds is the definition of insanity, but twenty-two out of twenty-four kids asked for a second serving. If that's not a ringing endorsement for a kid-favorite salad, I don't know what is!

1. In a medium salad bowl, combine carrots, parsley, and raisins. Toss to evenly distribute ingredients.

2. In a small bowl, whisk together olive oil, mustard, lemon juice, honey, salt, and pepper. Drizzle over carrot mixture and stir until well mixed. Refrigerate until ready to serve.

Calories: 90 | Fat: 5g | Protein: 1g | Sodium: 220mg | Fiber: 2g | Carbohydrates: 10g | Sugar: 7g | Added Sugar: 1g

1 pound fusilli pasta, cooked and drained

2 cups halved cherry tomatoes

1 medium cucumber, seeded and diced

½ medium red onion, peeled and diced

½ cup pitted and sliced California olives, drained

½ cup crumbled feta cheese

⅓ cup extra-virgin olive oil

⅛ cup white balsamic vinegar

2 cloves garlic, minced

1 tablespoon dried oregano

1 tablespoon dried thyme

½ teaspoon kosher salt

½ teaspoon freshly ground black pepper

MEDITERRANEAN PASTA SALAD

This chilled Mediterranean salad is perfect for when you need to feed a large crowd. It can easily be made the day before, and in fact, tastes better that way, as it gives all the flavors time to meld. Using white balsamic, instead of traditional balsamic, will let the vibrant colors of the dish shine through.

1. In a large serving bowl, combine pasta, tomatoes, cucumber, onion, olives, and feta.

2. In a small mixing bowl, whisk together oil, vinegar, garlic, oregano, thyme, salt, and pepper. Drizzle over pasta and toss well to coat.

3. Refrigerate at least 2 hours before serving.

Calories: 300 | Fat: 12g | Protein: 7g | Sodium: 340mg | Fiber: 1g | Carbohydrates: 41g | Sugar: 4g | Added Sugar: 0g

AVOCADO MANGO SALAD

Serves 6

PREP: 10 minutes
COOK: N/A

This brightly colored salad is both fresh and flavorful, a perfect way to welcome summer. When picking out fennel, opt for small bubs, about 2–3" in diameter, which are sweeter and crunchier than their larger counterparts. Also, make sure your mango and avocado are ripe but still slightly firm so they hold their shape.

1 tablespoon apple cider vinegar

1 tablespoon fresh lime juice

½ teaspoon salt

½ teaspoon freshly ground black pepper

2 tablespoons extra-virgin olive oil

2 medium mangos, peeled, pitted, and cubed

2 medium avocados, peeled, pitted, and cubed

1 small fennel bulb, very thinly sliced

½ cup chopped fresh cilantro leaves

1. In a small bowl, use a fork to whisk together vinegar, lime juice, salt, and pepper. Slowly whisk in olive oil.

2. In a large serving bowl, toss together mangos, avocado, fennel, and cilantro. Drizzle with vinegar–oil mixture and toss to coat. Serve immediately.

Calories: 200 | Fat: 12g | Protein: 2g | Sodium: 220mg | Fiber: 6g | Carbohydrates: 24g | Sugar: 17g | Added Sugar: 0g

3 tablespoons olive oil

3 tablespoons fresh lemon juice

1 teaspoon salt

½ teaspoon ground sumac

½ teaspoon freshly ground black pepper

1 pound Persian cucumbers, thinly sliced (unpeeled)

1 pint cherry tomatoes, quartered

1 cup minced fresh parsley

½ cup chopped fresh mint leaves

TOMATO CUCUMBER SALAD

I'm a firm believer that simple is better, especially when it comes to vegetables. After all, the simpler a dish is, the more likely we are to make it often. But don't get me wrong, simple doesn't mean flavorless. The key is to use fresh herbs and brightly acidic dressings (e.g., lemon juice) to bring out the best in a dish. This simple salad fits the bill and makes a light, refreshing pairing to just about any meal.

1. In a small bowl, use a fork to whisk together oil, lemon juice, salt, sumac, and pepper.

2. In a large serving bowl, toss together cucumber, tomato, parsley, and mint. Drizzle with olive oil mixture and toss to coat. Serve immediately or refrigerate up to 3 days.

Calories: 70 | Fat: 5g | Protein: 1g | Sodium: 250mg | Fiber: 1g | Carbohydrates: 5g | Sugar: 1g | Added Sugar: 0g

OIL AND VINEGAR COLESLAW

Serves 8

PREP: **5 minutes**
COOK: **N/A**

Creamy coleslaws may dominate most food menus, but oil and vinegar slaws like this one are light and refreshing, making them a great choice for hot summer days. The problem is, most oil and vinegar slaws call for a fair amount of sugar. Have no fear, this recipe uses just a bit of honey—about half of what most recipes call for—to add just enough sweetness to the dish.

¼ cup apple cider vinegar

1 tablespoon honey

2 tablespoons vegetable oil

1 (16-ounce) bag shredded cabbage mix

1 teaspoon salt

½ teaspoon freshly ground black pepper

1. In a large bowl, mix together vinegar and honey. Add oil. Add cabbage and toss, using your hands to massage the dressing into the slaw. Add salt and pepper; toss again.

2. Refrigerate at least 20 minutes to give the flavors time to meld before serving.

Calories: 50 | Fat: 3.5g | Protein: 1g | Sodium: 300mg | Fiber: 1g | Carbohydrates: 6g | Sugar: 4g | Added Sugar: 2g

Benefits of Cabbage

Cabbage is part of the cruci-ferous family, along with foods such as cauliflower, broccoli, and kale. In addition to helping play a role in reducing the risk of cancer, cabbage also has been shown to help suppress the inflammation that may lead to heart disease.

BROCCOLI APPLE SLAW

Serves 8

PREP: 10 minutes
COOK: N/A

Contrary to popular belief, research shows that kids prefer a variety of colors and textures on their plates rather than the monotone foods that most restaurant kid meals offer. This salad layers on the color and texture in a big way. You'll find green, orange, red, crunchy, crispy, and creamy all combined to create a flavor explosion perfect for a family get–together or picnic.

4 cups bite-sized fresh broccoli florets

1 medium carrot, peeled and sliced into thin coins

2 large Honeycrisp apples, cored and finely cubed

½ cup coarsely chopped walnuts, divided

1 cup raisins

1 cup plain nonfat Greek yogurt

2 tablespoons lemon juice

1 tablespoon pure maple syrup

¼ teaspoon kosher salt

½ teaspoon freshly ground black pepper

1. In a large bowl combine broccoli, carrots, apples, ¼ cup walnuts, and raisins.

2. In a small bowl, whisk together yogurt, lemon juice, syrup, salt, and pepper to make a salad dressing.

3. Add dressing to vegetables and toss to coat. Top with remaining ¼ cup walnuts. Chill until ready to serve.

Calories: 180 | Fat: 5g | Protein: 6g | Sodium: 105mg | Fiber: 4g | Carbohydrates: 29g | Sugar: 24g | Added Sugar: 2g

1 large bunch Tuscan kale

2 tablespoons olive oil

1 tablespoon balsamic vinegar

2 tablespoons fresh lemon juice

¼ teaspoon salt

¼ teaspoon freshly ground black pepper

¼ teaspoon crushed red pepper flakes

GRILLED KALE CHIPS

Who says potatoes get all the fun? Grilled kale chips are a great way to get kids to eat their greens. Unlike full kale leaves, which can resemble dinosaur food to kids, grilled kale is light and crispy. This recipe calls for a simple lemon and pepper topping, but you can get creative and use any toppings that you'd enjoy on potato chips.

1. Preheat oven to 350°F. Line a baking sheet with parchment paper.

2. Use a knife or kitchen shears to remove the kale leaves from the thick stems. Discard stems and cut leaves into bite-sized pieces. Transfer to the prepared baking sheet.

3. In a small bowl, whisk together oil, vinegar, lemon juice, salt, black pepper, and red pepper flakes. Pour vinaigrette over kale on baking sheet and use your hands to toss until kale is thoroughly coated.

4. Bake until edges are brown but not burnt, about 10–15 minutes. Serve immediately.

Calories: 70 | Fat: 7g | Protein: 1g | Sodium: 150mg | Fiber: 1g | Carbohydrates: 2g | Sugar: 1g | Added Sugar: 0g

SMASHED POTATO BITES

Serves 6

PREP: **10 minutes**
COOK: **75 minutes**

These potato bites combine the creaminess of mashed potatoes with the satisfying crispiness of fried potatoes. In this recipe you'll partially cook the potatoes on a baking sheet with a splash of water to get that coveted creamy texture. Be sure you let the potatoes rest after parcooking to help ensure they don't crumble apart when you smash them.

1 pound small (1–2"-diameter) red bliss potatoes, scrubbed clean

½ cup room-temperature water

3 tablespoons olive oil, divided

2 teaspoons Italian seasoning

1 teaspoon garlic powder

½ teaspoon sea salt

¼ teaspoon freshly ground black pepper

1. Preheat oven to 500°F.

2. Place potatoes on a rimmed baking sheet. Pour room-temperature water onto baking sheet and wrap tightly with aluminum foil.

3. Cook on bottom rack of oven until potatoes can be easily poked with a small knife, about 25–30 minutes. For ease, poke directly through the foil with your knife to test.

4. Remove foil and carefully blot potatoes and baking sheet dry with paper towels. Let cool 10–15 minutes.

5. Pour 1 tablespoon olive oil over potatoes; roll potatoes around to ensure they are well coated. Space potatoes evenly on baking sheet.

6. Use another rimmed baking sheet or a kitchen mallet to press down firmly on potatoes, flattening them to ½" thick.

7. Sprinkle with Italian seasoning, garlic powder, salt, and pepper. Drizzle with remaining olive oil.

8. Roast on middle rack until golden brown, about 35–45 minutes. Serve immediately.

A Quality Carbohydrate

When potatoes are prepared using healthy methods, they can fit into many different healthy eating patterns, including low-sugar, Mediterranean, and vegetarian eating plans. Potatoes provide important essential nutrients, including 45 percent of the daily value of vitamin C, as well as potassium and dietary fiber, two nutrients that are lacking in most people's diets.

Calories: 140 | Fat: 9g | Protein: 2g | Sodium: 280mg | Fiber: 0g | Carbohydrates: 13g | Sugar: 1g | Added Sugar: 0g

6 medium ears fresh corn, husked

2 teaspoons canola oil

2 cups halved cherry tomatoes

1 cup julienned fresh basil leaves

3 tablespoons lemon juice

¼ cup extra-virgin olive oil

1 teaspoon flaky sea salt

½ teaspoon freshly ground black pepper

GRILLED CORN SALAD

This colorful dish is full of simple summertime flavor. Be sure to grill the corn with the husks fully removed so you get that nice char on it. When you remove the kernels from the cob, use a sharp, serrated knife to remove the base of the cob, which will give you a nice flat surface to work with. Then, flip the corn so the flat surface meets your cutting board and use your knife to gently slide down the ear of corn to remove the kernels, being careful not to slice too close to the cob.

1. Rub corn with canola oil. Grill or broil 8 minutes or until kernels are lightly browned. Remove from heat and set aside to cool. Use a knife to remove kernels and place in a large serving bowl.

2. Add tomatoes and basil to bowl.

3. In a small bowl, whisk together lemon juice, oil, salt, and pepper. Drizzle dressing over vegetables and toss. Serve at room temperature.

Calories: 180 | Fat: 12g | Protein: 4g | Sodium: 400mg | Fiber: 3g | Carbohydrates: 20g | Sugar: 4g | Added Sugar: 0g

Serves 4

PREP: 10 minutes
COOK: 30 minutes

PARMESAN ZUCCHINI CHIPS

2 medium zucchini, sliced into
¼" rounds

1 tablespoon olive oil

½ cup freshly grated Parmesan
cheese

¼ cup whole-wheat panko

½ teaspoon garlic powder

¼ teaspoon freshly ground black
pepper

When fresh zucchini is in abundance, these zucchini "chips" are a breeze to make. Coated in a crispy Parmesan batter, it elevates seasonal zucchini to a whole new level. Make sure you slice the zucchini thinly for optimal crispiness. Enjoy them plain or serve with homemade Marinara Sauce (see Chapter 9) or Quick Ranch Dip (see Chapter 9) for dipping.

1. Preheat oven to 450°F. Line a baking sheet with parchment paper.

2. In a medium bowl, toss zucchini with oil.

3. In a small bowl, combine Parmesan, panko, garlic powder, and pepper. Dip each round into mixture, coating it evenly and using your fingers to help the mixture stick. Place in a single layer on the prepared baking sheet.

4. Bake until brown and crispy, about 20–30 minutes. Use a spatula to transfer to a serving plate and serve.

Calories: 110 | Fat: 7g | Protein: 5g | Sodium: 190mg | Fiber: 1g | Carbohydrates: 8g | Sugar: 2g | Added Sugar: 0g

SPAGHETTI SQUASH SAUTÉ

Serves 6

PREP: 10 minutes
COOK: 50 minutes

Cooked spaghetti squash has a texture similar to angel hair pasta: tender and chewy. On its own, the flavor is quite mild, but this means it can pair well with so many different flavors. This recipe keeps it simple with Parmesan, garlic, and black pepper. Think of this as the vegetable version of buttered noodles. Serve it with grilled chicken for a simple and satisfying meal.

1. Preheat oven to 350°F. Coat a rimmed baking sheet with cooking spray.

2. Place squash halves onto baking sheet, cut side down. Bake until squash is tender, about 40 minutes. Let cool 10–15 minutes.

3. Use a fork to scrape out squash flesh from rind into thin strips. Discard rind.

4. Melt butter in a medium skillet over medium heat. Lightly sauté garlic about 5 minutes until it softens but doesn't brown, stirring frequently. Add squash to skillet and stir to combine. Cook until squash is warmed, about 3–5 minutes.

5. Transfer squash to a medium serving bowl and season with salt and pepper. Top with Parmesan and chives. Serve immediately.

Calories: 190 | Fat: 8g | Protein: 4g | Sodium: 240mg | Fiber: 6g | Carbohydrates: 30g | Sugar: 12g | Added Sugar: 0g

Cooking spray

1 medium spaghetti squash, halved and seeded

3 tablespoons unsalted butter

1 clove garlic, finely minced

¼ teaspoon salt

½ teaspoon freshly ground black pepper

¼ cup freshly grated Parmesan cheese

2 tablespoons finely chopped fresh chives

MAPLE ACORN SQUASH

Serves 4

PREP: **10 minutes**
COOK: **30 minutes**

This is a quick, delicious, and beautiful side dish. By cutting the squash into slices, they look a bit like sunshine on your plate, a perfect pick-me-up for the doldrums of winter. Best of all, with just six ingredients that you likely have in your pantry, you can whip up a fancy-looking side dish with very little planning.

2 small acorn squashes

2 tablespoons olive oil

2 tablespoons pure maple syrup

1 tablespoon light brown sugar

½ teaspoon kosher salt

½ teaspoon freshly ground black pepper

1. Preheat oven to 400°F.

2. Cut squashes into ½"-thick slices. Use a round cookie cutter or sharp knife to cut out the pulpy portion of each slice so they resemble quarter-moons. Discard pulp.

3. Place squash on a rimmed baking sheet covered with parchment paper. Drizzle with olive oil and maple syrup; then sprinkle with brown sugar, salt, and pepper.

4. Roast 30 minutes or until tender and golden. Remove from oven and serve warm.

Calories: 180 | Fat: 7g | Protein: 2g | Sodium: 250mg | Fiber: 3g | Carbohydrates: 32g | Sugar: 8g | Added Sugar: 8g

4–5 large sweet potatoes, peeled and cut into 1" cubes

1 tablespoon coconut oil

1 tablespoon diced fresh chives

¼ cup whole milk

1 cup plain low-fat Greek yogurt

1 tablespoon pure maple syrup

1 teaspoon kosher salt

½ teaspoon freshly ground black pepper

SWEET POTATO MASH

Sweet potatoes are naturally sweet, making them a great way to curb sugar cravings without all the added sugar. This creamy mash makes for a great Thanksgiving side dish, but it is perfect any time of the year. While most people like to eat this dish warm, toddlers often seem to prefer it cold or at room temperature.

1. Add sweet potatoes to a large pot and add water to cover. Bring to a boil over high heat and boil about 25 minutes or until soft. Drain and place sweet potatoes in a large mixing bowl.

2. Add coconut oil, chives, milk, yogurt, maple syrup, salt, and pepper. Mash until combined, or use a hand mixer at low speed for a whipped consistency. Serve warm.

Calories: 160 | Fat: 3.5g | Protein: 7g | Sodium: 470mg | Fiber: 3g | Carbohydrates: 27g | Sugar: 9g | Added Sugar: 2g

Leading the Beta-Carotene Pack

Sweet potatoes, along with carrots, are leading sources of beta-carotene, a precursor to vitamin A, which is important for vision, skin health, and the immune system. Eating sweet potatoes and other beta-carotene-rich foods with a small amount of fat, such as coconut oil, milk, yogurt, or eggs, helps the body better absorb beta-carotene, compared to when the foods are eaten alone.

BAKED BEANS

Serves 8

PREP: 10 minutes
COOK: 45 minutes

Baked beans have a storied place in American culinary history, but most recipes typically have a hefty amount of sugar, usually from brown sugar, molasses, ketchup, and/or barbecue sauce. A traditional recipe might have 5–10 grams of added sugar per serving. This simple recipe lightens things up with just 2 grams added sugar and speeds along the cooking time by relying on canned, unsalted beans.

1. Preheat oven to 350°F.

2. Heat olive oil in a large ovenproof skillet over medium–low heat until warm, about 1 minute. Add onion, garlic, and green pepper to skillet; cook 3–4 minutes, stirring occasionally, until vegetables begin to soften.

3. Add soy sauce, water, syrup, vinegar, and paprika; increase heat to medium and bring to a simmer, stirring 2 minutes.

4. Add beans and tomato sauce; stir well. Transfer to oven and bake 30–40 minutes until sauce is thick.

5. Remove skillet from oven. Sprinkle beans with bacon and serve.

1 tablespoon olive oil

1 cup finely diced white onion

2 cloves garlic, minced

½ medium green bell pepper, seeded and finely diced

2 tablespoons low-sodium soy sauce

½ cup water

1 tablespoon pure maple syrup

1½ teaspoons apple cider vinegar

½ teaspoon smoked paprika

3 (15-ounce) cans unsalted navy beans

1 (8-ounce) can unsalted tomato sauce

4 slices low-sodium turkey bacon, cooked and chopped

Calories: 200 | Fat: 3g | Protein: 11g | Sodium: 200mg | Fiber: 10g | Carbohydrates: 32g | Sugar: 4g | Added Sugar: 2g

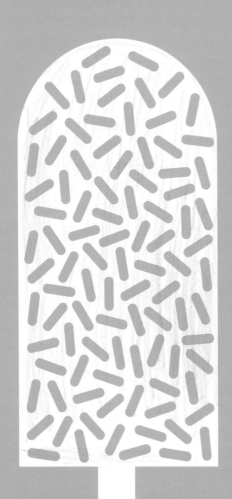

Chapter 8

DESSERTS

After sugar-sweetened beverages, desserts are (not surprisingly) the other major contributor of added sugar in the typical US diet. Collectively, desserts contribute about 20 grams of added sugar to the average person's diet. While you may be tempted to throw in the towel on desserts forever, not so fast. Banishing them altogether may leave your family feeling unnecessarily deprived, leading them to binge on sweets when they're away from your watchful eye. Luckily, the desserts in this chapter were developed to fit into your low-sugar lifestyle and keep everyone happy.

The desserts on the following pages all have about ⅓–½ of the sugar that you'd find in similar, traditional recipes. They feature smaller portion sizes, but are big on flavor, ensuring that you'll feel satisfied. And, unlike many store-bought desserts, they are completely free of artificial colors and preservatives.

Best of all, the meal plans in Appendix B will show you how you can enjoy a dessert every day while still coming in happily below the recommended limit for added sugar. You *can* have your cake and eat it too!

2 cups skim milk, divided

¼ teaspoon salt

2½ tablespoons cornstarch

1 teaspoon pure vanilla extract

¼ teaspoon pure almond extract

2 tablespoons honey

VANILLA PUDDING

A classic vanilla pudding is one of those satisfying pleasures of childhood, but like so many desserts, is often loaded with sugar. This creamy Vanilla Pudding is not only lower in sugar than classic store-bought brands, but gets its sweetness naturally, from honey. Serve it with mixed berries for a satisfying, nutrient-packed dessert.

1. Add 1½ cups milk to a medium saucepan over medium-high heat.

2. Meanwhile, in a medium bowl, whisk together salt, cornstarch, and ½ cup milk until cornstarch is dissolved, about 1 minute.

3. Add milk and cornstarch mixture to saucepan. Bring mixture to a boil, stirring constantly.

4. Continue to let mixture boil 2 minutes, stirring constantly. Reduce to a simmer and cook an additional 2–3 minutes.

5. Remove from heat. Stir in extracts and honey.

6. Let cool completely before transferring to a medium bowl. Cover with plastic wrap, making sure the plastic wrap touches the top of the pudding to prevent a film from forming. Refrigerate 3–4 hours or until thickened before serving.

Calories: 100 | Fat: 0g | Protein: 4g | Sodium: 210mg | Fiber: 0g | Carbohydrates: 19g | Sugar: 14g | Added Sugar: 8g

CHOCOLATE PUDDING

Chances are if you're not on team vanilla, then you're on team chocolate. This creamy Chocolate Pudding is made with rich, dark chocolate, unsweetened cocoa powder, and a reduced amount of sugar to indulge the chocolate lovers in your family while still staying on the lighter side of dessert.

1. In a medium bowl, whisk egg yolks until light yellow and thick, about 1 minute. Whisk in cornstarch and ¼ cup milk until smooth, about 1 minute. Set aside.

2. In a medium saucepan, heat sugar, cocoa powder, salt, and remaining milk over medium-high heat until gently simmering. Remove pan from heat and whisk into the egg mixture very slowly. (If you pour it in all at once, the eggs will scramble, and you don't want that.)

3. Once incorporated, return mixture to the saucepan and whisk in melted chocolate. Bring pudding to a boil, then reduce to a simmer. Whisk until pudding is thick, about 2–3 minutes.

4. Remove from heat and whisk in vanilla. Pour pudding into individual bowls or a medium bowl. Cover with plastic wrap, making sure the plastic wrap touches the top of the pudding to prevent a film from forming. Refrigerate at least 2 hours before serving.

2 large egg yolks

2 tablespoons cornstarch

2 cups skim milk, divided

3 tablespoons granulated sugar

¼ cup unsweetened cocoa powder

¼ teaspoon salt

4 ounces dark chocolate, melted

½ teaspoon pure vanilla extract

Calories: 290 | Fat: 15g | Protein: 9g | Sodium: 220mg | Fiber: 2g | Carbohydrates: 33g | Sugar: 20g | Added Sugar: 7g

VANILLA CAKE WITH BERRIES AND CREAM

This is a great cake for sharing with a group of family and friends. It's beautiful, light, and fluffy—a perfect taste of summer. Most traditional frosted, layered cakes have a whopping 50 grams of added sugar or more. This scrumptious beauty has a fraction of that, totaling just 11 grams of added sugar. But, don't worry, it's still full of flavor, thanks to the sour cream, lemon zest, and fresh, juicy berries.

CAKE
2 teaspoons butter (for greasing pans)

2 heaping tablespoons all-purpose flour (for greasing pans)

2¾ cups unbleached cake flour

1 cup granulated sugar

1 tablespoon baking powder

¾ teaspoon salt

¾ cup unsalted butter, softened

4 large egg whites

1 whole large egg

1 cup sour cream

1 tablespoon pure vanilla extract

2 teaspoons lemon zest

1. Preheat oven to 350°F. Prepare 2 (8") round pans by greasing bottom and sides of each with 1 teaspoon butter, then coating each with 1 heaping tablespoon all-purpose flour. Turn pans upside down and shake off any excess flour, then set pans aside.

2. In a stand mixer with paddle attachment, mix together cake flour, sugar, baking powder, and salt on low until well combined, about 30 seconds. Add softened butter and mix until a fine crumble forms, 3–4 minutes.

3. Add egg whites, one at a time, then the whole egg. Be sure to continue to beat well after each addition, scraping down the sides of the bowl with a spatula to incorporate all ingredients.

4. In a small bowl, whisk together sour cream, vanilla, and lemon zest. Add mixture ⅓ at a time to batter, mixing at low speed about 30 seconds after each addition, stopping to scrape down the sides of the bowl with a spatula. Keep beating until nice and fluffy, about 2 more minutes.

5. Pour batter into prepared pans, dividing it equally. Use a spatula to even out the batter in the pans. Bake on the center rack of the oven 20–25 minutes or until a toothpick inserted in the center comes out clean. »

(continued on page 166)

BERRIES AND CREAM

2 cups heavy cream, chilled

3 tablespoons granulated sugar

1 teaspoon pure vanilla extract

1 pint fresh strawberries, hulled
and thinly sliced

1 pint fresh blueberries

6. Remove from oven and let cakes rest in pans about 5 minutes. Then, carefully remove from pans and cool on a wire rack at least 30 minutes.

7. To make cream frosting, whip cream, sugar, and vanilla in a stand mixer fitted with whisk attachment on medium speed until firm, about 8–10 minutes.

8. Place one cake on a cake stand or serving platter and use a spatula to spread half the whipped cream on top. Scatter with half the strawberries and blueberries.

9. Carefully place remaining cake on top and use a spatula to spread remaining whipped cream on top.

10. To make a "flower" shape on top, place overlapping strawberry slices around the top of the cake, starting near the outer edge and working in for a total of three rows. Fill in the center with blueberries. Sprinkle remaining fruit around cake on platter. Refrigerate until ready to serve. Best if eaten within 1–2 days.

. . . .

Calories: 360 | Fat: 23g | Protein: 5g | Sodium: 160mg | Fiber: 1g | Carbohydrates: 36g | Sugar: 16g | Added Sugar: 11g

VANILLA CUPCAKES

Serves 12
(serving size: 1 cupcake)

PREP: 10 minutes
COOK: 25 minutes

There's nothing more classic than Vanilla Cupcakes. Perfect for birthday parties and other celebrations, this light and fluffy recipe is sweet and golden, beating out any boxed mix. Keep it classic by topping it with Vanilla Frosting or mix things up and top it with Double Chocolate Frosting (see recipes in this chapter). Let the cupcakes cool at least 30 minutes after removing them from the pan before frosting them.

1¼ cups all-purpose flour

1 teaspoon baking powder

¼ teaspoon salt

½ cup unsalted butter, softened

1 cup granulated sugar

2 large eggs

2 teaspoons pure vanilla extract

½ cup light sour cream

1. Preheat oven to 350°F. Line a 12-cup muffin pan with paper liners.

2. Sift together flour, baking powder, and salt in a large bowl.

3. In a medium bowl, whisk together butter, sugar, eggs, vanilla, and sour cream until combined.

4. Add butter mixture to the bowl with the flour mixture, stirring to combine well.

5. Divide batter equally among the lined muffin cups, filling each ⅔ of the way full. Bake 25 minutes or until a toothpick inserted in the center comes out clean. Let cool 5 minutes, then remove from muffin pan.

Calories: 180 | Fat: 10g | Protein: 3g | Sodium: 260mg | Fiber: 0g | Carbohydrates: 23g | Sugar: 12g | Added Sugar: 12g

1½ cups all-purpose flour

⅓ cup unsweetened cocoa powder

1½ teaspoons baking soda

¼ teaspoon salt

1 cup granulated sugar

1¼ cups light sour cream

⅔ cup vegetable oil

2 large eggs

1½ teaspoons pure vanilla extract

1 teaspoon espresso powder

CHOCOLATE CUPCAKES

These soft and moist Chocolate Cupcakes are absolutely irresistible. The recipe uses unsweetened cocoa powder to help bring down the added sugar to a more reasonable amount than traditional cupcakes. And using just a sprinkle of espresso powder gives the cupcakes a deep richness that will make chocolate lovers everywhere rejoice!

1. Preheat oven to 350°F. Line a 12-cup muffin pan with paper liners.

2. Sift together flour, cocoa powder, baking soda, and salt into a large bowl.

3. In a medium bowl, whisk together sugar, sour cream, oil, eggs, vanilla, and espresso powder until combined.

4. Add the sugar mixture to the flour mixture, stirring to combine well.

5. Divide batter equally among the lined muffin cups, filling each ⅔ of the way full. Bake 25 minutes or until a toothpick inserted in the center comes out clean. Let cool 5 minutes, and then remove from muffin pan.

Calories: 260 | Fat: 16g | Protein: 4g | Sodium: 240mg | Fiber: 16g | Carbohydrates: 27g | Sugar: 12g | Added Sugar: 12g

STRERY CUPCAKES

Serves 12
(serving size: 1 cupcake)

PREP: 10 minutes
COOK: 25 minutes

When it comes to cupcakes, vanilla and chocolate shouldn't have all the fun! Strawberries are one of kids' favorite fruits, so it's no surprise that blending them into cupcakes makes for a delicious, kid-friendly treat. Top these light, moist cupcakes with Strawberry Frosting (see recipe in this chapter) for a whimsical, pinkalicious treat. Be sure to let the cupcakes cool at least 30 minutes after you remove them from the muffin pan before frosting them.

2¼ cups fresh strawberries, hulled and chopped

¾ cup skim milk

6 large egg whites

1½ teaspoons pure vanilla extract

2¼ cups all-purpose flour

1 cup granulated sugar

4 teaspoons baking powder

½ teaspoon salt

¾ cup unsalted butter, cubed and softened

1. Preheat oven to 350°F. Line a 12-cup muffin pan with paper liners. Set aside.

2. Add strawberries to a blender or food processor and purée until smooth, about 2 minutes. Strain mixture, reserving solids for frosting, if using.

3. Place strawberry juice in a small saucepan over medium-high heat. Bring to a boil and cook until thick and syrupy, about 6–8 minutes. Whisk milk into juice.

4. In a large bowl, whisk together egg whites, vanilla, and strawberry-milk mixture.

5. In a separate large bowl, whisk together flour, sugar, baking powder, and salt. Add butter one piece at a time and beat in with an electric mixer on medium-low speed about 3 minutes. Add half the wet ingredients and beat until light and fluffy, about 1 minute. Add the rest of the wet ingredients and beat until incorporated, about 2 minutes.

6. Divide batter equally among the lined muffin cups, filling each ⅔ full. Bake 20–25 minutes or until a toothpick inserted in the center comes out clean. Let cool 5 minutes, and then remove from muffin pan.

Calories: 250 | Fat: 12g | Protein: 5g | Sodium: 135mg | Fiber: 1g | Carbohydrates: 33g | Sugar: 14g | Added Sugar: 12g

VANILLA FROSTING

Serves 8
(serving size: 2 tablespoons)

PREP: 5 minutes
COOK: N/A

Take a look at the ingredients label for most store-bought frostings and you'll see a long list of artificial flavors and dyes, including Yellow 5 and Red 40. Don't settle for the fake stuff when you can whip together your own luscious version with just a few ingredients. Your taste buds and body will be glad you did!

½ cup unsalted butter, softened

1 cup confectioners' sugar

2 teaspoons pure vanilla extract

2 tablespoons skim milk

1. Beat butter on medium speed with stand mixer or electric mixer until smooth, about 2 minutes.

2. Add sugar and vanilla, beating until well combined, about 2 minutes.

3. Drizzle in the milk and beat until smooth, about 1 minute. Use immediately to frost a cake or cupcakes, or store in an airtight container in the refrigerator up to 2 weeks.

Calories: 160 | Fat: 11g | Protein: 0g | Sodium: 0mg | Fiber: 0g | Carbohydrates: 15g | Sugar: 15g | Added Sugar: 14g

1¼ cups unsalted butter, softened

1 cup confectioners' sugar

¾ cup unsweetened cocoa powder

¼ teaspoon salt

½ cup honey

1 teaspoon pure vanilla extract

11 ounces dark chocolate, melted and cooled

DOUBLE CHOCOLATE FROSTING

If you're a chocolate lover, this recipe is for you. Using both unsweetened cocoa powder and dark chocolate, it packs a double chocolate punch to satisfy your most ravenous chocolate cravings. This frosting can be stored in an airtight container in the refrigerator up to 2 weeks.

1. Add butter, sugar, cocoa, and salt to the bowl of a stand mixer. Beat on medium speed until combined well, about 2 minutes.

2. Add honey and vanilla, beating on medium-low until combined well, about 1 minute.

3. Add chocolate and beat on medium-low until smooth, about 2 minutes. Use immediately to frost a cake or cupcakes, or store in the refrigerator.

Calories: 170 | Fat: 13g | Protein: 1g | Sodium: 25mg | Fiber: 1g | Carbohydrates: 15g | Sugar: 11g | Added Sugar: 8g

STRAWBERRY FROSTING

This creamy Strawberry Frosting is simplicity at its best. Made with puréed fresh strawberries and cream cheese, it's smooth, creamy, and beautifully colored, without any artificial food dyes. Enjoy it spread on your favorite cake or cupcakes to make a perfectly pink dessert for any pink lovers in your family.

¾ cup unsalted butter, softened

2 cups confectioners' sugar

12 ounces cream cheese, cubed and softened

2¼ cups fresh strawberries, hulled, puréed, juices drained

¼ teaspoon salt

1. Beat butter and sugar in a stand mixer at medium-low speed until pale and fluffy, about 2–3 minutes.

2. Add cream cheese, beating on medium-low speed until incorporated, about 2 minutes.

3. Add puréed strawberries and salt. Beat on low speed until combined, about 1 minute. Use immediately to frost a cake or cupcakes, or store in an airtight container in refrigerator up to 2 weeks.

Calories: 110 | Fat: 8g | Protein: 1g | Sodium: 50mg | Fiber: 0g | Carbohydrates: 9g | Sugar: 8g | Added Sugar: 7g

1½ cups hulled and chopped fresh strawberries

2 tablespoons honey

1 teaspoon fresh lemon zest

½ teaspoon pure vanilla extract

1 cup heavy cream, chilled

STRAWBERRY MOUSSE

Strawberry mousse is a light, creamy dessert that makes good use of fresh strawberries when they're in summertime abundance. If fresh strawberries aren't in season, feel free to use frozen strawberries, which are typically frozen at their peak of freshness. Just be sure to properly thaw and drain the frozen berries before you use them in the recipe so you don't end up with a watery mousse.

1. In a food processor or blender, purée strawberries, honey, lemon zest, and vanilla until smooth. Set aside.

2. In the bowl of a stand mixer using whisk attachment, whisk heavy cream on medium speed until it reaches stiff peaks, about 8–10 minutes. Gently fold in the strawberry purée until just incorporated.

3. Divide the mixture into 4 serving bowls and cover with plastic wrap. Chill at least 2 hours before serving.

Calories: 250 | Fat: 22g | Protein: 2g | Sodium: 15mg | Fiber: 1g | Carbohydrates: 14g | Sugar: 12g | Added Sugar: 8g

STRAWBERRY ALMOND TARTLETS

Serves 12

PREP: 15 minutes
COOK: 8 minutes

These bite-sized tartlets feature a wholesome almond and whole-wheat crust, topped with fresh, juicy berries. They are elegant enough to impress at a party (think baby shower or bridal shower) while still being super simple to make. And with just 4 grams added sugar per serving, they have just a fraction of what's in most traditional party desserts.

4 teaspoons unsalted butter, melted, divided

2 cups dry-roasted unsalted almonds

3 tablespoons honey, divided

2 tablespoons whole-wheat flour

1 teaspoon ground ginger

¼ teaspoon salt

1 pound fresh strawberries, sliced

1 teaspoon lemon juice

1. Grease a 12-cup muffin pan with 2 teaspoons melted butter.

2. Pulse almonds in a food processor until coarsely ground.

3. Add 2 tablespoons honey, flour, ginger, salt, and remaining butter to the food processor. Process until a coarse dough forms, then gather into a ball.

4. Press 1 heaping tablespoon dough along the bottom and up the sides of each muffin cup. Chill in the refrigerator 1 hour.

5. Preheat oven to 350°F.

6. Bake crusts 8 minutes or until firm and golden around edges. Let cool in pan 10 minutes, then remove.

7. Add strawberries, lemon juice, and remaining honey to a medium bowl. Stir well to release the juices from the strawberries.

8. Fill each crust with the strawberry mixture and serve.

Calories: 180 | Fat: 14g | Protein: 5g | Sodium: 50mg | Fiber: 3g | Carbohydrates: 13g | Sugar: 7g | Added Sugar: 4g

CINNAMON-SPIKED "DOUGHNUTS"

Cooking spray
1½ cups whole-wheat flour
1 tablespoon ground cinnamon
½ teaspoon baking soda
½ teaspoon baking powder
¼ teaspoon salt
½ cup pure maple syrup
1 large egg, beaten
½ cup 2% milk
2 teaspoons pure vanilla extract
1 tablespoon coconut oil, melted

This treat has all the taste of cinnamon doughnuts but with half the mess. The secret: the cinnamon is baked directly into them rather than dusted on the outside. Since most people don't own doughnut tins, this recipe relies on a mini muffin tin to shape the scrumptious little bites. An alternative is to use a cake pop machine, if you have one.

1. Preheat oven to 350°F. Spray a 30-cup mini muffin pan with cooking spray.

2. In a medium bowl, whisk together flour, cinnamon, baking soda, baking powder, and salt.

3. In a small bowl, combine syrup, egg, milk, and vanilla; mix thoroughly, about 1 minute. Slowly drizzle in coconut oil and mix well, about 1 minute.

4. Slowly add wet ingredients to dry ingredients and mix until just combined, about 1–2 minutes.

5. Spoon the batter equally into the prepared muffin pan, about 1–2 tablespoons per cup.

6. Bake 10 minutes. Remove from oven and let cool in pan 5 minutes. Serve warm.

Calories: 90 | Fat: 1.5g | Protein: 2g | Sodium: 90mg | Fiber: 2g | Carbohydrates: 17g | Sugar: 7g | Added Sugar: 7g

Cooking spray

⅓ cup honey

½ cup unsalted butter, softened

1 cup whole-wheat flour

¼ teaspoon baking soda

¼ teaspoon salt

¾ cup rolled oats

¾ cup Raspberry Jam (see Chapter 9)

RASPBERRY OAT BARS

These little raspberry bars are packed with flavor and are easy to make. The best part is, unlike so many other baked goods, there's only one bowl and one pan to clean in the end. Made with seven simple ingredients, including honey, whole-wheat flour, and oats, this is a treat you can feel good about giving your kids. Use a low-sugar store-bought raspberry jam or follow the Raspberry Jam recipe (see Chapter 9) to make your own.

1. Preheat oven to 350°F. Grease a 9" × 13" sheet pan thoroughly with cooking spray, including the corners.

2. In a mixer with a paddle attachment, combine honey and butter; mix on low until fully combined, about 2 minutes. Turn mixer off and scrape down sides of the bowl to make sure all the butter is incorporated.

3. Add flour, baking soda, salt, and oats to the butter and mix on low until crumbles start to form, about 3–4 minutes. You don't want to overmix or the dough may become tough. If you are mixing the dough without a mixer, use your hands to incorporate the butter into the flour to make a crumble.

4. Add about half the dough crumbles to the prepared pan. Use your hands to spread it out evenly along the bottom of the pan, pressing it down firmly. The idea here is to make a crust on the bottom of the pan, so don't be afraid to press down hard.

5. Scoop jam over the top of the dough in the pan. Use a spatula to spread it out evenly over the dough.

6. Sprinkle the remaining dough over the top of the jelly to make a crumble layer.

7. Bake 30–40 minutes. Let cool, then cut into 1" × 1" squares. These will keep 3–4 days at room temperature, 2 weeks in the refrigerator, or 1 month in the freezer.

Calories: 90 | Fat: 4g | Protein: 1g | Sodium: 40mg | Fiber: 1g | Carbohydrates: 13g | Sugar: 6g | Added Sugar: 6g

CHOCOLATE CHIP MINI COOKIES

Serves 20
(serving size: 1 cookie)

PREP: 15 minutes
COOK: 12 minutes

Chocolate chip cookies are a classic favorite. This recipe helps you enjoy them even as you strive to follow a low-sugar diet. Featuring whole-wheat flour and just a few tablespoons brown sugar, this recipe rings in at 3 grams added sugar per serving, just a fraction of a traditional cookie. If you like chewy cookies, err toward the shorter cooking time, but if you prefer crisper cookies, lean toward the longer baking time.

1 large egg

1 tablespoon pure vanilla extract

5 tablespoons brown sugar

½ cup coconut oil, melted

1½ cups whole-wheat flour

½ teaspoon salt

½ teaspoon ground cinnamon

½ cup dark chocolate chips

1. In a stand mixer with a paddle attachment, combine egg, vanilla, sugar, and coconut oil and mix on low speed until combined, about 2 minutes.

2. Add flour, salt, and cinnamon to the mixer and continue mixing on low just until combined and a dough forms, about 2 minutes.

3. Add chocolate chips and stir in by hand.

4. Line a baking sheet with parchment paper. Scoop cookie dough into balls about 1" in diameter and place on baking sheet. Squish each ball slightly to flatten.

5. Refrigerate cookies on baking sheet at least 2 hours. (Chilling the dough will help ensure even baking and result in a cookie with a chewier center.)

6. Remove cookies from refrigerator and preheat oven to 350°F.

7. Bake 8–12 minutes. Transfer cookies to a wire rack and let cool about 30 minutes. Store in an airtight container up to 1 week.

Calories: 110 | Fat: 7g | Protein: 2g | Sodium: 60mg | Fiber: 1g | Carbohydrates: 11g | Sugar: 5g | Added Sugar: 3g

¼ cup coconut oil

½ cup pure maple syrup

1 teaspoon pure vanilla extract

2 large egg whites

⅔ cup all-purpose flour

½ teaspoon baking powder

½ teaspoon salt

¼ cup dark chocolate chips, melted

¼ cup diced fresh strawberries

STRAWBERRY FUDGE COOKIES

Fudge cookies are tasty on their own, but add in some fresh strawberries and it takes the flavor quotient up a big notch. I like to make these when fresh strawberries are beginning to turn. My kids don't like to eat strawberries that are anything less than perfect, so it's a great way to use berries that are no longer at their peak of freshness.

1. Preheat oven to 350°F. Line a baking sheet with parchment paper.

2. In a medium bowl, cream together oil, syrup, and vanilla.

3. Add egg whites and whisk until mixture is smooth, about 1–2 minutes.

4. In a large bowl, sift together flour, baking powder, and salt. Add wet ingredients to dry ingredients in four parts. Mix with a rubber spatula to combine.

5. Add melted chocolate to the mixture and use spatula to mix until just combined, about 30 seconds. The mixture will be thick and viscous.

6. Gently fold in strawberries.

7. Drop by the tablespoonful onto the prepared baking sheet to make 12 cookies, placing them about 2" apart. Bake 15 minutes or until cookies have puffed up. Transfer cookies to a wire rack and let cool about 30 minutes. Store in an airtight container up to 1 week.

Calories: 120 | Fat: 6g | Protein: 2g | Sodium: 110mg | Fiber: 0g | Carbohydrates: 17g | Sugar: 10g | Added Sugar: 8g

LEMON CORNMEAL COOKIES

Serves 48
(serving size: 1 cookie)

PREP: 15 minutes
COOK: 15 minutes

This recipe make a perfect little lemon cookie flavored with the wholesome taste of cornmeal and honey. I like to use a mini ice cream scoop to scoop the dough for these cookies; a number 100 scoop works great, which is the size of about a teaspoon. This makes cookies that are small enough to pop into your mouth in just one or two bites, helping you keep portion sizes in check.

¾ cup unsalted butter, softened

Zest of 2 medium lemons

¼ cup granulated sugar

⅓ cup honey

1 large egg

1 teaspoon pure vanilla extract

1½ cups all-purpose flour

1 cup cornmeal

½ teaspoon baking soda

1 teaspoon salt

1. Preheat oven to 350°F. Line a baking sheet with parchment paper.

2. In a stand mixer with paddle attachment, mix the softened butter, lemon zest, sugar, and honey on low until fully combined, about 2 minutes.

3. Add egg and vanilla to mixer, scraping down the bowl to ensure all the ingredients are incorporated.

4. Add flour, cornmeal, baking soda, and salt to the mixer and allow all the ingredients to come together in a nice dough, about 2 minutes.

5. Scoop the dough by the teaspoonful onto the prepared baking sheet to make 48 cookies. Leave only about 1" between each cookie, as they will not spread too much.

6. Bake 15 minutes or until the cookies are golden brown on the edges. Transfer cookies to a wire rack and let cool about 30 minutes. Store in an airtight container up to 1 week.

Calories: 70 | Fat: 3g | Protein: 1g | Sodium: 65mg | Fiber: 0g | Carbohydrates: 9g | Sugar: 3g | Added Sugar: 3g

OATMEAL CHERRY COOKIES

Serves 24
(serving size: 1 cookie)

PREP: 15 minutes
COOK: 14 minutes

These Oatmeal Cherry Cookies are a flavorful, wholesome twist on an iconic favorite. The ingredient list features all-natural, nourishing ingredients including rolled oats, whole-wheat flour, coconut oil, dried cherries, and cinnamon. Go ahead and make a double batch to share with a friend or a new mom (or be selfish and freeze some for you to enjoy another day!).

1. Preheat oven to 325°F. Line a baking sheet with parchment paper.

2. In a large bowl, whisk egg. Add dried cherries and set aside to soak 15 minutes.

3. In a stand mixer with a whisk attachment, whisk together coconut oil, honey, and vanilla on low speed, about 1 minute.

4. Add the cherry mixture to oil mixture and whisk together on low speed, about 1 minute.

5. Add oats, flour, baking powder, baking soda, cinnamon, and salt. Mix on low speed until a nice dough forms, about 2 minutes.

6. Scoop out about 2 tablespoons dough and form into a ball. Flatten slightly with the palm of your hand and place on the prepared baking sheet. Repeat with the remaining dough to make 24 cookies, placing them about 2" apart.

7. Bake 12–14 minutes. Transfer cookies to a wire rack and let cool about 30 minutes. Enjoy warm or store in an airtight container up to 1 week.

Calories: 70 | Fat: 2g | Protein: 1g | Sodium: 40mg | Fiber: 1g | Carbohydrates: 13g | Sugar: 6g | Added Sugar: 5g

1 large egg

½ cup unsweetened dried cherries

2 tablespoons coconut oil

½ cup honey

2 teaspoons pure vanilla extract

1 cup rolled oats

¾ cup whole-wheat flour

1½ teaspoons baking powder

¼ teaspoon baking soda

1¾ teaspoons ground cinnamon

¼ teaspoon salt

The Benefits of Dried Cherries

Dried cherries are a perfect combination of sweet and tart, making them a great flavor addition to baked goods. But they also have nutritional benefits. Dried cherries are rich in antioxidants and nutrients that support heart health and reduce overall inflammation.

Nonstick baking spray (to grease muffin pan)

6 tablespoons unsalted butter

1¼ cups semisweet chocolate chips

2 teaspoons pure vanilla extract

2 large eggs

1½ tablespoons unsweetened cocoa powder

1 cup tapioca flour

½ cup granulated sugar

½ teaspoon salt

BROWNIE BITES

These amazing bite-sized treats are rich and chocolatey with just a hint of sweetness to satisy any cravings. This recipe uses tapioca flour, in lieu of traditional wheat flour, making them a great gluten-free option for anyone with allergies or sensitivities. I like to store any leftovers in an airtight container in the freezer, then pop one or two in the microwave after dinner for the perfect cap to a meal.

1. Preheat oven to 350°F. Grease a 24-cup mini muffin pan liberally with nonstick baking spray.

2. In a small saucepan over low heat, melt butter, about 2 minutes. Once melted, add chocolate chips and stir until melted, about 1 minute. Remove from heat and pour into a medium mixing bowl; let cool slightly, 1–2 minutes.

3. Add vanilla and eggs to mixing bowl; mix thoroughly, about 1 minute.

4. Sift cocoa powder and tapioca flour into the bowl with the chocolate mixture. Add sugar and salt; mix everything together well, about 2 minutes.

5. Pour batter into the prepared pan using a tablespoon to divide it equally among the muffin cups. Bake 18–20 minutes. Allow brownies to cool in pan, and then serve or transfer to an airtight container. Store up to 1 week in refrigerator or 2 months in freezer.

Calories: 110 | Fat: 6g | Protein: 1g | Sodium: 55mg | Fiber: 1g | Carbohydrates: 14g | Sugar: 9g | Added Sugar: 9g

Serves 24
(serving size: 1 bar)

PREP: 10 minutes
COOK: 90 seconds

2½ cups unsweetened shredded coconut

⅓ cup coconut butter, melted

¼ cup honey

⅛ teaspoon salt

½ teaspoon pure vanilla extract

¼ teaspoon pure almond extract

1 tablespoon coconut oil, melted

8 ounces dark chocolate, roughly chopped

CHOCOLATE COCONUT BARS

This candy bar is inspired by Mounds bars but features all-natural ingredients, including coconut, coconut butter, honey, and dark chocolate. It's a slightly more sophisticated take on the packaged original, but is just as scrumptious—and has just 3 grams added sugar per bar. Because the recipe is low in sugar and preservative-free, these are best stored in the refrigerator.

1. In a medium bowl, stir together shredded coconut, coconut butter, honey, salt, extracts, and coconut oil.

2. Use your hands to form mixture into 24 small balls.

3. Line a rimmed baking sheet with wax paper. Add candy bars to the baking sheet and freeze 15–30 minutes or until firm and set.

4. Add chocolate to a microwavable bowl. Heat on high in the microwave in 30-second increments until melted, stirring between cooking times, about 90 seconds total.

5. Dip candy bars in the chocolate and return to the baking sheet. Chill another 5 minutes in the freezer until the chocolate is set. Store in the refrigerator.

Calories: 130 | Fat: 10g | Protein: 1g | Sodium: 20mg | Fiber: 1g | Carbohydrates: 11g | Sugar: 8g | Added Sugar: 3g

CINNAMON BAKED APPLE

Serves 1

PREP: **5 minutes**
COOK: **45 minutes**

This Cinnamon Baked Apple is dessert the way nature intended. But don't be fooled by the simple ingredient list; it's a warm, comforting treat that tastes way more indulgent than it really is. Tip: put the apple into the oven to bake before you sit down for dinner so that dessert is ready when you are. And be sure to double, triple, or quadruple the recipe so everyone in your home can enjoy.

1 teaspoon unsalted butter, melted

1 teaspoon light brown sugar

¼ teaspoon ground cinnamon

2 tablespoons chopped pecans

1 tablespoon raisins

1 medium Honeycrisp apple, cored to create a 2" diameter hole in center

1. Preheat oven to 375°F.

2. In a small mixing bowl, combine butter, sugar, cinnamon, pecans, and raisins.

3. Place the apple in an 8" × 8" glass baking dish and stuff with the cinnamon mixture.

4. Bake 35–45 minutes until tender.

5. Remove from oven and let cool 10 minutes. Enjoy warm.

Calories: 270 | Fat: 14g | Protein: 2g | Sodium: 10mg | Fiber: 7g | Carbohydrates: 40g | Sugar: 31g | Added Sugar: 4g

MINI APPLE PIES

Serves 18
(serving size: 1 pie)

PREP: 10 minutes
COOK: 18 minutes

A classic American pie gets a nutritional upgrade in this recipe with whole-wheat flour and honey. Better yet, the mini serving size helps to ensure that everyone gets an appropriately portioned piece. While the recipe calls for Granny Smith apples, feel free to substitute them for McIntosh, Golden Delicious, Ambrosia, or any combination that suits your fancy.

1. Preheat oven to 350°F. Grease 18 cups of a mini muffin pan with melted coconut oil.

2. In a large bowl, stir together flour, baking powder, salt, cinnamon, nutmeg, ⅓ cup honey, and butter until loosely combined, about 1 minute. Use your hands to help the butter further mix into the dough by pressing the butter between your fingers. This will break it up into fine crumbs.

3. Add about 2 teaspoons dough to each muffin cup, using about half the dough. Press dough firmly into the bottom of the cups.

4. In a medium bowl, stir together apples, cornstarch, vanilla, lemon zest, and remaining 1 tablespoon honey. Add about 1½ teaspoons filling to each muffin cup.

5. Top each cup with remaining dough crumbles, about 2 teaspoons per cup, pressing down into the cups.

6. Bake 15–18 minutes until golden brown. Let cool 5 minutes before removing from the muffin pan. Serve warm.

Calories: 90 | Fat: 4g | Protein: 1g | Sodium: 35mg | Fiber: 1g | Carbohydrates: 13g | Sugar: 7g | Added Sugar: 6g

1 tablespoon coconut oil, melted

1 cup whole-wheat flour

¾ teaspoon baking powder

⅛ teaspoon salt

½ teaspoon ground cinnamon

¼ teaspoon ground nutmeg

⅓ cup plus 1 tablespoon honey, divided

4½ tablespoons cold unsalted butter, cut into small cubes

1¼ cups diced, peeled Granny Smith apples

1¼ teaspoons cornstarch

½ teaspoon pure vanilla extract

¼ teaspoon lemon zest

An Apple a Day

All varieties of apples are rich in important antioxidants, flavonoids, and dietary fiber. Research has shown that these phytonutrients may help reduce the risk of cancer, hypertension, diabetes, and heart disease. Additionally, apples are a good source of immune-boosting vitamin C and have been shown to aid in weight loss.

½ cup almond butter

2 tablespoons agave syrup

1 tablespoon almond flour

14 large pitted Medjool dates

⅓ cup water

¼ teaspoon salt

¼ teaspoon pure vanilla extract

⅓ teaspoon pure almond extract

1 tablespoon coconut oil, melted

⅓ cup chopped unsalted peanuts

1 cup dark chocolate chips

PEANUT NOUGAT CANDY BARS

Hungry? Whip up a healthier take on the classic Snickers bar. Unlike the highly processed original, this recipe relies on natural sweeteners such as agave syrup and Medjool dates to create the caramel and nougat goodness that's oh-so-popular. The result: a satisfying and delicious twist on the original with just 1 gram added sugar per serving.

1. To make the nougat, stir together almond butter, agave, and almond flour until combined. Press the nougat filling onto a baking sheet lined with parchment paper, creating a rectangle that is about ½" thick. Freeze 10 minutes to set.

2. To make the caramel, combine dates, water, salt, vanilla extract, almond extract, and coconut oil in a blender or food processor and purée until smooth, about 1–2 minutes.

3. Spread caramel on top of the layer of nougat. Sprinkle chopped peanuts on top, gently pressing them into the caramel. Freeze 35 minutes to set.

4. Add chocolate chips to a microwavable bowl. Heat on high in the microwave in 30-second increments until melted, stirring between cooking times, about 90 seconds total.

5. Remove candy from freezer and cut into 24 miniature candy bars.

6. Dip candy bars in the chocolate and return to the baking sheet. Chill another 10 minutes in the freezer until the chocolate is set. Store in the freezer.

Calories: 160 | Fat: 7g | Protein: 3g | Sodium: 35mg | Fiber: 2g | Carbohydrates: 24g | Sugar: 20g | Added Sugar: 1g

MINI PEANUT BARS

Serves 24
(serving size: 1 bar)

PREP: 5 minutes
COOK: 10 minutes

If you love peanuts, you are going to go bonkers over this easy candy bar reinvention. The miniature size makes for a perfectly portioned bite-sized dessert. And because it's packed with peanuts, it's more filling and satisfying than a carb-based dessert. Store any leftovers in an airtight ≠container in the refrigerator up to a week.

1. Grease an 8" × 8" baking pan with ½ tablespoon butter, coating the sides and bottom. Add half the peanuts to pan.

2. Stir together peanut butter and 1½ tablespoons butter in a large saucepan over medium heat until melted.

3. Stir in condensed milk and marshmallows. Cook until melted, stirring constantly, about 3 minutes.

4. Pour mixture evenly over the peanuts in the baking pan.

5. Top with remaining peanuts.

6. Let cool about 30 minutes. Cut into 24 miniature bars and store in refrigerator.

2 tablespoons unsalted butter, divided

20 ounces unsalted roasted peanuts, divided

8 ounces natural creamy peanut butter

12 ounces sweetened condensed milk

1½ cups mini marshmallows

Calories: 260 | Fat: 19g | Protein: 9g | Sodium: 45mg | Fiber: 3g | Carbohydrates: 17g | Sugar: 11g | Added Sugar: 2g

6 ounces dark chocolate chips

1½ cups dry-roasted unsalted almonds

1 teaspoon flaky sea salt, such as Maldon salt

CHOCOLATE ALMOND CLUSTERS

These three-ingredient Chocolate Almond Clusters are highly addictive, but with no added sugar, you can go ahead and indulge in one or two pieces, guilt-free. Make sure you use a high-quality dark chocolate with at least 70% cocoa to get the most benefits out of the dark chocolate. Keep any remaining clusters in an airtight container in the refrigerator up to 2 weeks or in the freezer up to 3 months.

1. Line a baking sheet with parchment paper.

2. Place chocolate chips in a small microwave-safe bowl. Microwave on 50 percent power in 30-second increments, stirring between cooking times until chocolate is about two-thirds melted, about 60 seconds total. Remove from microwave and stir until fully melted.

3. Add almonds. Stir until each almond is coated in chocolate.

4. Use a spoon to scoop clusters onto the prepared baking sheet, aiming for about 2 tablespoons per cluster. Sprinkle with sea salt.

5. Refrigerate 30 minutes or until the clusters are firm.

Calories: 190 | Fat: 14g | Protein: 4g | Sodium: 190mg | Fiber: 2g | Carbohydrates: 12g | Sugar: 7g | Added Sugar: 5g

DARK CHOCOLATE–DIPPED STRAWBERRIES

Serves 12
(serving size: 1 strawberry)

PREP: 10 minutes
COOK: 1 minute

Chocolate-covered strawberries not only look impressive, but are also a cinch to make. Nutritional bonus: the strawberries and dark chocolate together make for an antioxidant power-house. As with many recipes in this book, this recipe is simple enough to make with your child, helping to spark a lifelong love of cooking.

¾ cup dark chocolate chips

12 large fresh strawberries

1. Line a baking sheet with parchment paper.

2. Place chocolate chips in a small microwave-safe bowl. Microwave on 50 percent power in 30-second increments, stirring between cooking times until chocolate is about two-thirds melted, about 60 seconds total. Remove from microwave and stir until fully melted.

3. Dip strawberries one at a time into dark chocolate, holding onto the leaves and swirling until fully coated. Shake off excess chocolate and gently place on parchment paper. Repeat with remaining strawberries.

4. Refrigerate 30 minutes or until chocolate is hardened. Enjoy the same day. While they're okay to eat for a few days, they won't look as pretty.

The Antioxidant Power of Dark Chocolate

Dark chocolate contains polyphenols, which act as a powerful antioxidant in reducing blood pressure and free-radical damage in the body. To get the most benefit, select dark chocolate with a 70% or higher total cocoa content and enjoy it in moderation.

Calories: 50 | Fat: 2g | Protein: 1g | Sodium: 0mg | Fiber: 0g | Carbohydrates: 6g | Sugar: 2g | Added Sugar: 1g

½ cup almond flour

¼ cup tapioca flour

5 tablespoons cold unsalted butter

2 teaspoons honey

¾ teaspoon pure vanilla extract

2 tablespoons dark chocolate chips

¼ teaspoon flaky sea salt

CHOCOLATE CHIP COOKIE DOUGH

This creamy, edible Chocolate Chip Cookie Dough tastes just like the real thing, but has way less sugar and is meant to be eaten straight out of the mixing bowl. Featuring dark chocolate chips, honey, and a combination of almond and tapioca flours, you can feel good about letting your kids lick the spoon!

Combine almond flour, tapioca flour, butter, honey, and vanilla in a blender and blend until smooth. Stir in the chocolate and salt. Serve immediately.

Calories: 270 | Fat: 22g | Protein: 3g | Sodium: 150mg | Fiber: 2g | Carbohydrates: 15g | Sugar: 4g | Added Sugar: 3g

MINT CHOCOLATE CHIP "ICE CREAM"

Serves 2

PREP: 5 minutes
COOK: N/A

This three-ingredient ice cream is clean, simple, and refreshing. While it's dairy-free and has no added sugar, it still feels like an indulgent treat. To make sure you're always prepared to make this anytime your kids scream for ice cream, keep frozen sliced bananas ready to go in the freezer.

2 ripe medium bananas, peeled, sliced, and frozen

¼ cup chopped fresh mint

¼ cup dark chocolate chips

1. Add bananas and mint to food processor and blend about 1 minute. Scrape down the sides using a spatula and continue to blend until smooth, about 3 minutes.

2. Scoop into a medium bowl and mix in dark chocolate. Enjoy immediately, or for a firmer ice cream, place in an airtight, freezer-safe container and freeze 1 hour.

More Ice Cream Flavors

The flavor options are endless for this banana-style "ice cream." Try swapping out the mint with 1–2 tablespoons peanut butter. Or add freshly diced berries or cherries. For some crunch, add a few nuts, some granola, or even pretzels.

Calories: 190 | Fat: 4.5g | Protein: 2g | Sodium: 0mg | Fiber: 3g | Carbohydrates: 36g | Sugar: 16g | Added Sugar: 3g

2 medium oranges, peeled and sectioned

1½ cups unsweetened coconut milk

2 tablespoons honey

1 teaspoon pure vanilla extract

ORANGE CREAM POPS

There's something about orange cream ice pops that define a happy summer. These pops are made with fresh oranges instead of juice, which give them a brighter flavor and a bit more fiber. Fruit-based pops are also a great way to help kids rehydrate if they're too preoccupied to drink water or feel a bit under the weather.

1. Lay orange sections flat on a baking sheet and freeze 30 minutes.

2. In a blender, blend half of the frozen orange sections and all the coconut milk until smooth, about 1 minute. Add the remaining orange slices, honey, and vanilla and blend until smooth, about 1 minute.

3. Pour into 6 ice-pop molds and insert ice-pop sticks into each. Freeze until solid, about 2–3 hours.

Calories: 60 | Fat: 1g | Protein: 0g | Sodium: 0mg | Fiber: 1g | Carbohydrates: 11g | Sugar: 9g | Added Sugar: 5g

CHOCOLATE PEANUT BUTTER POPS

Serves 6

PREP: 5 minutes
COOK: N/A

These super creamy pops bring together the favorite flavor duo of rich chocolate and smooth peanut butter. With virtually no added sugar, these treats can be enjoyed any time of day, even for breakfast. Just don't tell your kids they're snacking on 100 percent wholesome ingredients! Store any uneaten pops in the freezer up to a month.

1 large banana, peeled and sliced

½ cup unsweetened almond milk

¼ cup plain low-fat Greek yogurt

1 tablespoon natural creamy peanut butter

½ teaspoon pure vanilla extract

2 tablespoons unsweetened cocoa powder

1. Combine all ingredients in a blender and blend until smooth, about 1 minute.

2. Pour into 6 ice-pop molds and insert ice-pop sticks into each. Freeze until solid, about 2–3 hours.

Calories: 50 | Fat: 2g | Protein: 2g | Sodium: 25mg | Fiber: 1g | Carbohydrates: 7g | Sugar: 3g | Added Sugar: 0g

1 pint fresh blueberries
3 tablespoons honey, divided
1 cup plain low-fat Greek yogurt
¼ cup nonfat milk
1 pint fresh raspberries

ROCKET POPS

These red, white, and blue pops have serious patriotic flair and are totally free of the artificial dyes that color the store-bought version. They look best when you make them in a rocket-shaped ice-pop mold, but they'll still look gorgeous in a classic-style ice-pop mold. The layering and freezing process takes a little extra time, but it's totally worth the effort.

1. Place blueberries and 1 tablespoon honey in a blender and purée until smooth, about 1 minute.

2. Pour the blueberry purée into 6 ice-pop molds, dividing it equally among them so each mold is about ⅓ full. Place pops in freezer to set, about 30 minutes.

3. Combine yogurt, milk, and 1 tablespoon honey in a medium bowl. Whisk until smooth, about 30 seconds.

4. Pour the yogurt mixture into the ice-pop molds on top of the blueberry mixture, dividing it equally among them so each mold is about ⅔ full. Place pops in freezer to set, about 30 minutes.

5. Place raspberries and remaining 1 tablespoon honey in a blender and blend until smooth, about 1 minute. Pour over the yogurt mixture in the molds, dividing it equally among them.

6. Finish the pops by placing sticks in each mold and freezing until set, about 2–3 hours.

Calories: 120 | Fat: 1.5g | Protein: 6g | Sodium: 25mg | Fiber: 4g | Carbohydrates: 23g | Sugar: 17g | Added Sugar: 8g

DIPS, SAUCES, AND SPREADS

Limiting added sugars in sugar-sweetened beverages and candy bars may seem obvious. But added sugar can be sneaky, popping into a lot of different foods where you might not expect it. For example, almost one-fourth of a traditional ketchup bottle is filled with sugar, usually in the form of high-fructose corn syrup. And, just 2 tablespoons of traditional barbecue sauce can have as much as 10 grams of sugar!

The recipes in this chapter will show you how you can make your own dips, sauces, and spreads with just a fraction of the sugar. A side perk: most of these recipes are much easier to make than you might think, making them perfect "starter" recipes to involve your little budding chefs in the kitchen.

Another benefit to making your own dips and sauces? You can feel confident about every ingredient that goes into them and wow your friends and family in the process.

16 ounces dry-roasted unsalted
peanuts
½ teaspoon salt
2 tablespoons peanut oil

PEANUT BUTTER

Homemade creamy peanut butter is one of those ultimate comfort foods. The good news is, it's way easier to make than you might think. All you really need is a food processor, peanuts, a touch of salt, and a drizzle of peanut oil. Unlike many store-bought peanut butters, this recipe has no added sugar. Spread it on a slice of whole-grain toast, and if you're craving a touch of sweetness, top it with fresh sliced strawberries for a nourishing breakfast or snack.

1. Place peanuts in the bowl of a food processor and process 3 minutes, stopping to scrape down the sides of the bowl every minute or so.

2. Add salt and peanut oil. Continue to process about 2–5 minutes until peanut butter reaches desired consistency, scraping down the sides of the bowl as needed. Scoop peanut butter into an airtight container and store in the refrigerator up to 2 months.

Calories: 190 | Fat: 17g | Protein: 7g | Sodium: 80mg | Fiber: 3g | Carbohydrates: 6g | Sugar: 1g | Added Sugar: 0g

RASPBERRY JAM

Truth be told, fruit jams need a fair amount of sugar to help create that jam-like consistency. However, this three-ingredient recipe uses the minimal amount of sugar—in the form of honey—that's needed to still create a true jam. Try it on whole-grain sprouted toast or homemade corn muffins.

1 pound raspberries (about 4 cups)

⅔ cup honey

1 teaspoon lemon juice

1. Combine all ingredients in a medium Dutch oven. Bring to a boil over medium-high heat. Reduce heat to medium and allow mixture to continue to boil, stirring and using a spatula to scrape down the sides of the pot occasionally, about 40 minutes.

2. To check doneness, place a plate in the refrigerator to cool about 10 minutes, then dribble small droplets of hot jam on the plate. The droplets will "set up" and immediately have a jam-like consistency when fully cooked.

3. Strain jam through a fine-meshed strainer to remove seeds if desired. Refrigerate in an airtight container up to 2–3 weeks.

Calories: 25 | Fat: 0g | Protein: 0g | Sodium: 0mg | Fiber: 1g | Carbohydrates: 7g | Sugar: 6g | Added Sugar: 5g

CHOCOLATE HAZELNUT SPREAD

Serves 7
(serving size: 2 tablespoons)

PREP: 10 minutes
COOK: 5 minutes

Chocolate Hazelnut Spread is a classic treat, but unfortunately the store-bought versions are loaded with sugar. This all-natural version uses much less sugar, allowing the earthy taste of hazelnuts and the rich taste of cocoa powder to shine through. Spread it on whole-grain toast for a satisfying snack without the guilt.

1 cup shelled hazelnuts

2 teaspoons pure vanilla extract

⅛ cup unsweetened cocoa powder

2 tablespoons pure maple syrup

½ teaspoon salt

1 teaspoon vegetable oil

¼ cup unsweetened almond milk

1. Preheat oven to 400°F. Place hazelnuts on a rimmed baking sheet and roast about 5 minutes, being careful not to burn.

2. Rub the hazelnuts together in a paper towel to remove most of the skins.

3. In a food processor, blend the nuts until they form a butter consistency. This may take up to 5 minutes.

4. Add remaining ingredients and blend an additional 2 minutes, stopping to scrape down the sides of the bowl using a spatula, until it's nice and creamy. Store in refrigerator up to 2 weeks.

Calories: 120 | Fat: 10g | Protein: 2g | Sodium: 160mg | Fiber: 2g | Carbohydrates: 6g | Sugar: 4g | Added Sugar: 3g

4 ounces low-fat cream cheese

½ cup hulled and roughly
chopped fresh strawberries

1 teaspoon honey

STRAWBERRY CREAM CHEESE SPREAD

Strawberry Cream Cheese Spread is a simple treat that can be easily made at home, saving you from extra preservatives and artificial colors. This recipe uses fresh, natural ingredients to create a spread that your whole family can enjoy guilt-free. If fresh strawberries aren't in season, go ahead and use frozen strawberries; just be sure to defrost and drain them first.

Place all ingredients in the bowl of food processor and blend until smooth, about 2–3 minutes. Serve immediately or refrigerate in an airtight container up to 3 days.

Calories: 40 | Fat: 2.5g | Protein: 1g | Sodium: 65mg | Fiber: 0g | Carbohydrates: 3g | Sugar: 2g | Added Sugar: 1g

RASPBERRY DIP

Serves 7
(serving size: 2 tablespoons)

PREP: 5 minutes
COOK: N/A

This Raspberry Dip, featuring just three all-natural ingredients, is the perfect accompaniment to a fresh fruit platter. If you want to add even more kid-appeal, put sliced fruit onto wooden skewers, alternating colors to create a vibrant fruit kabob. Then serve with this luscious Raspberry Dip and let kids dip away!

½ cup raspberries
½ cup plain low-fat Greek yogurt
1 tablespoon honey

Blend all ingredients in a food processor until smooth, about 1–2 minutes. Or, simply mash all the ingredients in a small bowl until well combined. Store in a mason jar up to a week.

Calories: 30 | Fat: 0g | Protein: 2g | Sodium: 5mg | Fiber: 1g | Carbohydrates: 4g | Sugar: 3g | Added Sugar: 2g

¾ cup plain low-fat Greek yogurt

2 tablespoons honey

2 tablespoons yellow mustard

1 tablespoon Dijon mustard

1 tablespoon lemon juice

¼ teaspoon ground cayenne pepper

HONEY MUSTARD DIP

This Honey Mustard Dip has just a little bit of kick to help balance out the sweetness and tanginess of the honey and mustard. Enjoy it spread on your favorite sandwich or use it as a dip for Whole-Grain Pretzel Bites (see Chapter 5). Store it in an airtight container in the refrigerator up to 1 week.

Combine all ingredients in a small bowl; stir well. Cover and chill 2–3 hours.

Calories: 30 | Fat: 0.5g | Protein: 2g | Sodium: 75mg | Fiber: 0g | Carbohydrates: 5g | Sugar: 4g | Added Sugar: 3g

SPICY PEANUT DIP

Serves 10
(serving size: 2 tablespoons)

PREP: 10 minutes
COOK: 10 minutes

This Spicy Peanut Dip is inspired by traditional Thai peanut dips, which marry creamy peanut butter with spicy red pepper and salty soy sauce. Use this dip as an accompaniment to fresh vegetable slices or the Vegetable Spring Rolls (see Chapter 4). Or serve over grilled chicken, steamed broccoli, and brown rice.

1. Heat oil in a medium nonstick skillet over medium heat. Add shallot, garlic, and ginger and sauté 3 minutes, stirring frequently.

2. Add red pepper flakes, followed by water, peanut butter, lime juice, soy sauce, and sugar. Use a fork to gently whisk together ingredients. Simmer 3–5 minutes until mixture thickens, stirring constantly. Season with salt.

3. Transfer to a bowl and let cool 1–2 hours at room temperature to allow flavors to continue to meld. Serve chilled or at room temperature.

Calories: 150 | Fat: 13g | Protein: 5g | Sodium: 140mg | Fiber: 2g | Carbohydrates: 5g | Sugar: 2g | Added Sugar: 0g

1 tablespoon vegetable oil

1 large shallot, peeled and finely minced

1 clove garlic, finely minced

2 teaspoons finely minced fresh ginger

¼ teaspoon crushed red pepper flakes

1 cup water

½ cup natural creamy peanut butter

1 tablespoon fresh lime juice

1 tablespoon low-sodium soy sauce

1 teaspoon light brown sugar

¼ teaspoon salt

1 cup plain low-fat Greek yogurt

1 teaspoon dried dill

1 teaspoon dried chives

1 teaspoon garlic powder

1 teaspoon dried parsley

1 teaspoon dry mustard

2 teaspoons lemon juice

½ teaspoon salt

¼ teaspoon freshly ground black pepper

QUICK RANCH DIP

Research has shown that kids are 80 percent more likely to eat bitter vegetables, such as broccoli, when they're served with dip. That's good news, but unfortunately most store-bought dips use added sugars as a leading ingredient. This recipe is a big hit with my kids, has zero added sugar, and is a breeze to make. Serve this dip with a plate of veggies or toasted pita chips.

Combine all ingredients in a medium bowl and mix well. Serve immediately or store in an airtight container in the refrigerator up to a week.

Calories: 25 | Fat: 0.5g | Protein: 3g | Sodium: 125mg | Fiber: 0g | Carbohydrates: 2g | Sugar: 1g | Added Sugar: 0g

Turn It Into Ranch Dressing

If you'd like to use this dip as a salad dressing, simply thin out the dip with 1–2 tablespoons olive oil. Slowly whisk in the olive oil once all ingredients are mixed until the consistency is just right.

HERBY TAHINI DIP

1 cup packed chopped fresh
flat-leaf Italian parsley

¼ cup packed chopped fresh mint

¼ cup packed chopped fresh dill

1 clove garlic, minced

3 tablespoons tahini

2 tablespoons fresh lemon juice

2 tablespoons cold water, divided

1 tablespoon olive oil

¼ teaspoon salt

Health Benefits of Herbs

Fresh herbs, such as parsley, basil, cilantro, mint, oregano, and others, not only add fresh flavor and aroma to foods, allowing you to cut back on sodium and sugar, but they also have amazing medicinal properties. Herbs have a number of potent anti-oxidants, called polyphenols, that have been shown to help combat a number of diseases including cancer, heart disease, Alzheimer's, diabetes, and more.

This refreshing green dip uses tahini as the base. Tahini is a paste made from ground sesame seeds, most often used as one of the key ingredients in hummus. While this dip is reminiscent of hummus, it's filled with fresh herbs rather than the chickpeas of traditional hummus. The result is a bold, green dip that pairs well with just about everything, from veggies and crackers to scrambled eggs and burgers.

1. Place parsley, mint, dill, and garlic in the bowl of a food processor; process 1 minute.

2. Add tahini and lemon juice. Continue to process until a paste begins to form, about 1–2 minutes, scraping down the sides of the bowl as necessary.

3. Add 1 tablespoon water, olive oil, and salt. Continue to process until desired consistency is reached, scraping down sides of bowl as necessary and adding the remaining tablespoon of water if desired.

4. Transfer to a serving bowl and serve immediately, or place in an airtight container and refrigerate up to 1 week or freeze up to 3 months.

Calories: 80 | Fat: 7g | Protein: 2g | Sodium: 115mg | Fiber: 1g | Carbohydrates: 3g | Sugar: 0g | Added Sugar: 0g

CUCUMBER MINT YOGURT DIP

Serves 20
(serving size: 2 tablespoons)

PREP: 5 minutes
COOK: N/A

This dip, inspired by Greek tzatziki, goes great with grilled chicken and rice. But don't stop there. Serve it with a platter of veggies and pita slices for an appetizer or afternoon snack. Or pack a small container in your child's lunch with a side of fresh-cut veggies. Enjoy it within 1 week for optimal freshness.

1. Lay diced cucumbers on two layers of paper towels and top with another two layers of paper towels; gently squeeze to push out any water. Allow cucumber to continue to drain for 30 minutes.

2. In a medium bowl, mix cucumber, yogurt, garlic, mint, dill, lemon juice, and salt. Refrigerate 2 hours to allow flavors to meld before serving.

Calories: 10 | Fat: 0g | Protein: 2g | Sodium: 35mg | Fiber: 0g | Carbohydrates: 1g | Sugar: 1g | Added Sugar: 0g

1 medium cucumber, peeled, seeded, and finely diced

1½ cups plain nonfat Greek yogurt

1 clove garlic, finely minced

1 tablespoon finely chopped fresh mint

1 tablespoon finely chopped fresh dill

1 tablespoon fresh lemon juice

¼ teaspoon salt

2 medium avocados

1 clove garlic, finely minced

1 tablespoon finely chopped scallions

¼ cup coarsely chopped fresh cilantro leaves

1 tablespoon fresh lime juice

¼ teaspoon coarse sea salt

The Nutrient Booster

Heart-healthy avocados provide nearly twenty essential nutrients, including potassium, vitamin E, folate, and fiber. They also act as a nutrient booster by enabling the body to absorb more fat-soluble nutrients, such as beta-carotene and lutein, in foods that are eaten with avocados.

SIMPLE GUACAMOLE

Everybody loves fresh guacamole. The good news is, it's so simple to make, even a kid could do it, making this a great recipe for budding chefs. Be sure to use perfectly ripe avocados. The best way to tell if an avocado is ready is to gently squeeze it; a ready-to-eat avocado will be firm yet yield to gentle pressure. If you don't plan to serve the guacamole immediately, cover it with plastic wrap so that the plastic wrap is directly on the surface of the guacamole and refrigerate until ready to serve.

1. Cut avocados in half, remove pits, and scoop flesh into a medium mixing bowl.

2. Add garlic, scallions, cilantro, and lime. Use a fork to mash everything together. Season with salt and mix well. Scoop into a serving bowl and serve immediately.

Calories: 45 | Fat: 4g | Protein: 1g | Sodium: 60mg | Fiber: 2g | Carbohydrates: 3g | Sugar: 0g | Added Sugar: 0g

CLASSIC HUMMUS

Serves 20
(serving size: 2 tablespoons)

PREP: 5 minutes
COOK: N/A

This recipe is a loose adaptation of my Lebanese grandmother's hummus. If you love garlic, go ahead and add 1 or 2 more cloves to the recipe, but I've kept this recipe on the mild side to make it more appealing to kids. Serve it with fresh vegetable slices and warm, fresh pita. Or use it in a sandwich, in lieu of mayonnaise.

1 (16-ounce) can unsalted chickpeas, drained and rinsed

2 tablespoons tahini

½ cup water, divided

¼ cup fresh lemon juice

1 clove garlic, roughly chopped

¼ teaspoon salt

1 tablespoon olive oil

1 teaspoon ground sumac

1. Add chickpeas, tahini, and ¼ cup water to the bowl of a food processor. Blend 1–2 minutes, scraping down the sides of the mixing bowl with a spatula as needed.

2. Add lemon juice and pulse 30 seconds.

3. Slowly add remaining water while pulsing until consistency is smooth, about 1 minute.

4. Add garlic and salt and blend another 30 seconds.

5. Transfer to a serving bowl, drizzle with olive oil, and sprinkle with sumac.

Calories: 40 | Fat: 1.5g | Protein: 1g | Sodium: 35mg | Fiber: 1g | Carbohydrates: 4g | Sugar: 0g | Added Sugar: 0g

1 (6-ounce) can unsalted tomato paste

½ cup water

1 tablespoon white distilled vinegar

½ teaspoon salt

½ teaspoon garlic powder

HOMEMADE KETCHUP

Many popular ketchup brands use high-fructose corn syrup as a leading ingredient. Skip the sugar altogether and make your own, faster than you'd even be able to get through the supermarket checkout line. Enjoy it with burgers, Smashed Potato Bites (see Chapter 7), or use it as the base for homemade barbecue sauce or other favorite sauces that call for ketchup.

1. Mix all ingredients in a medium saucepan and bring to a boil over medium-high heat.

2. When ketchup comes to a boil, reduce heat to medium-low and simmer 10 minutes, stirring frequently.

3. Remove from heat and let cool. Transfer to a lidded glass jar and store in refrigerator up to 2 weeks.

Calories: 10 | Fat: 0g | Protein: 1g | Sodium: 110mg | Fiber: 1g | Carbohydrates: 3g | Sugar: 2g | Added Sugar: 0g

SWEET AND TANGY BARBECUE SAUCE

Serves 8
(serving size: 2 tablespoons)

PREP: 5 minutes
COOK: 35 minutes

Most barbecue sauces are loaded with sugar. This sweet and tangy version has about half the amount you'll find in many barbecue sauces, making it a good transition recipe to help your family's taste buds adjust to lower-sugar foods. Serve it with Simple BBQ Chicken Sliders (see Chapter 6) or on top of your favorite burger.

2 teaspoons olive oil

¼ medium yellow onion, peeled and finely diced

1 clove garlic, finely diced

1 tablespoon tomato paste

1 (8-ounce) can unsalted tomato purée

½ teaspoon ground turmeric

2 tablespoons light brown sugar

2 tablespoons apple cider vinegar

1 tablespoon pure maple syrup

1 teaspoon dry mustard

1 tablespoon low-sodium soy sauce

½ teaspoon chili powder

½ teaspoon smoked paprika

1 teaspoon liquid smoke

1. Add olive oil to a medium saucepan over medium heat. Add onion and cook until soft, about 3–5 minutes. Add garlic and cook 2 minutes, stirring frequently.

2. Reduce heat to low and mix in all remaining ingredients. Simmer 30 minutes, stirring frequently.

3. Transfer to a medium mixing bowl and use an immersion blender to blend until smooth, about 1–2 minutes. Alternately, you can use a high-powered blender. Refrigerate sauce in an airtight container up to 2 weeks or freeze up to 3 months.

Calories: 45 | Fat: 1.5g | Protein: 1g | Sodium: 115mg | Fiber: 1g | Carbohydrates: 9g | Sugar: 7g | Added Sugar: 5g

1 tablespoon olive oil

1 small yellow onion, peeled and finely diced

1 medium carrot, peeled and diced

2 cloves garlic, finely minced

1 (28-ounce) can unsalted whole peeled tomatoes

1 tablespoon dried oregano

¼ teaspoon salt

¼ teaspoon freshly ground black pepper

¼ cup roughly chopped fresh basil leaves

MARINARA SAUCE

Many jarred marinara sauces have added sugar as a leading ingredient. Rather than rely on processed sugars, this simple recipe gets a touch of sweetness the natural way, from a finely diced carrot. Make a double batch and freeze whatever you don't plan to eat now so that you're well stocked for a busy day. Marinara sauce obviously goes great with a variety of pastas and pizza, but you can also simmer fried eggs in it, use it as a sandwich dip, or use it to amp up the flavor of freshly steamed veggies.

1. Warm olive oil in a medium saucepan over medium heat. Add onions and sauté until softened, about 5 minutes. Stir in carrots and garlic and sauté another 1 minute.

2. Add tomatoes with juices to saucepan. Use a spatula to gently smash them against the pan to begin to break them up.

3. Add oregano, salt, and pepper. Increase heat to medium-high to bring sauce to a simmer. Lower heat to medium-low to maintain the simmer until sauce is slightly thickened, about 20 minutes. Stir in fresh basil, remove from heat, and serve. Store leftovers in airtight container up to a week.

Calories: 45 | Fat: 1.5g | Protein: 1g | Sodium: 80mg | Fiber: 1g | Carbohydrates: 4g | Sugar: 3g | Added Sugar: 0g

BREAKFAST CEREAL REFERENCE GUIDE

Ready-to-eat breakfast cereals have many practical benefits: they are affordable, quick to get on the table, require almost no cleanup, and are generally well-liked. Unfortunately, many are loaded with sugar, negating the benefits. Luckily, with more than one hundred kinds of cereal in most grocery stores, there are several that can fit into your low-sugar lifestyle.

The following nutrition criteria can help you make smart choices.

Calories ≤ 200	In general, your child's breakfast cereal should have around 200 calories or less per serving. This allows for the addition of milk and fruit, while still remaining within a reasonable calorie range for the day. When reading the nutrition facts to determine the calories, don't forget to check out the serving size. A serving size of cereal can vary from ½ cup to more than 1 cup. If you know that your child generally eats more than ½ cup of a given cereal and that cereal has a relatively high calorie count, it's time to find a better alternative.
Total Sugar ≤ 6 grams	In general, opt for cereals that have 6 grams or less of total sugar. When reading the ingredient list, be wary of cereals that have multiple forms of sugar (e.g., evaporated cane juice, fruit juice concentrate). Also, many times cereals use dried fruit that has been coated in sugar. It's better to simply add your own unsweetened dried fruit. If your child's favorite cereal is slightly higher than this amount, try mixing it with another no-sugar or low-sugar option. This can also be a good strategy to use as your child transitions to a lower-sugar way of life.
Fiber ≥ 5 grams	Choose a cereal with at least 5 grams of fiber to help your child meet the recommended daily value of 25 grams and feel full until lunchtime. In addition to reading the nutrition facts label for the fiber amount, look for first ingredients such as 100% whole wheat, oats, or another grain. If the front of the box says "whole grain" then at least half the grain ingredients are whole. If it says "100% whole grain" it means that all the grain ingredients are whole grain. If your child's favorite cereal is low in sugar, but also low in fiber, add your own toppings to help boost the fiber content, such as fresh fruit, nuts, flaxseeds, or chia seeds.
No artificial colors or flavors	Some cereals use artificial colors to give cereal a colorful kid-appeal. However, research has shown that about 15 percent of the population may be sensitive to these dyes, resulting in hyperactivity or attention problems. It's best to avoid them altogether. Likewise, some cereals use artificial sweeteners such as sucralose and acesulfame potassium as a way to reduce the sugar and/or calorie content. Again, there is some evidence linking these ingredients to potential negative health effects, making it best to avoid them.

SAMPLE MEAL PLANS

In Chapter 1 we talked about how most kids should limit their added sugar intake to 25 grams or less per day. The following meal plans demonstrate how you can accomplish that goal using recipes in this book, accompanied by simple fresh fruit, vegetables, and other staples.

All the following meal plans are between 1,400 and 1,600 calories per day, which is appropriate for kids ages four through eight who are moderately active. If you have a tween or teen, especially one who is very active, her calorie intake will be higher than this. If your child needs more calories to meet her energy needs, she can increase her portion sizes and/or add another snack to her daily meal plan. If your child needs fewer calories (i.e., children younger than four or children who are sedentary), go ahead and decrease the portion sizes accordingly.

SUMMER MEAL PLAN (1,560 calories; 21 grams added sugar)

Meal	Recipe	Calories	Added Sugar (grams)
Breakfast:	Peachy Cream Pancakes	300	9
Morning Snack:	Chocolate Peanut Butter Protein Bars	180	6
Lunch:	Greek Tortellini Salad	450	0
Afternoon Snack:	Cucumber Boats	110	1
Dinner:	Grilled Margarita Pizza	340	1
Dessert:	Strawberry Almond Tartlets	180	4

FALL MEAL PLAN (1,440 calories; 16 grams added sugar)

Meal	Recipe	Calories	Added Sugar (grams)
Breakfast:	Whole-Grain Pumpkin Waffles	240	6
Morning Snack:	Oatmeal Cookie Energy Bites	190	3
Lunch:	Apple Cheddar Melt	490	0
Afternoon Snack:	Slow Cooker Applesauce	100	0
Dinner:	Alphabet Minestrone Soup	230	0
	1 whole-wheat dinner roll	100	0
Dessert:	Cinnamon-Spiked "Doughnuts"	90	7

WINTER MEAL PLAN (1,415 calories; 21 grams added sugar)

Meal	Recipe	Calories	Added Sugar (grams)
Breakfast:	Banana Walnut Baked Oatmeal	320	6
Morning Snack:	1 clementine orange	35	0
Lunch:	Sweet Potato and Spinach Quesadillas	450	0
Afternoon Snack:	Graham Crackers	130	7
	Healthier Hot Cocoa	50	4
Dinner:	Smoky Lentil Soup	160	0
Dessert:	Cinnamon Baked Apple	270	4

SPRING MEAL PLAN (1,430 calories; 15 grams added sugar)

Meal	Recipe	Calories	Added Sugar (grams)
Breakfast:	Wild Blueberry–Stuffed French Toast	330	0
Morning Snack:	Chocolate Zucchini Bread	140	9
Lunch:	Cucumber Tea Sandwiches	260	0
Afternoon Snack:	20 almonds	150	0
	½ cup grapes	50	0
Dinner:	Orecchiette with Roasted Broccoli, Tomatoes, and Walnuts	410	0
Dessert:	Raspberry Oat Bars	90	6

VEGETARIAN MEAL PLAN (1,450 calories; 22 grams added sugar)

Meal	Recipe	Calories	Added Sugar (grams)
Breakfast:	Green Monster Smoothie	120	0
	Cranberry Date Energy Bites	160	2
Morning Snack:	1 apple	95	0
	Peanut Butter	190	0
Lunch:	Vegetable Spring Rolls	130	0
	Spicy Peanut Dip	150	0
Afternoon Snack:	2 Corn Bread Mini Muffins	160	10
	Raspberry Jam	25	5
Dinner:	Veggie Lasagna Cups	150	0
	1 whole-wheat dinner roll	100	0
	Simple mixed green salad with vinaigrette	100	0
Dessert:	Oatmeal Cherry Cookies	70	5

(continued >>)

MEDITERRANEAN MEAL PLAN (1,425 calories; 15 grams added sugar)

Meal	Recipe	Calories	Added Sugar (grams)
Breakfast:	Cheesy Egg Cups	160	0
Morning Snack:	1 apricot	50	0
	String cheese	80	0
Lunch:	Baked Falafel Bites	170	0
	Whole-wheat pita bread	175	0
	Classic Hummus	40	0
	½ cup sliced cucumber	15	0
Afternoon Snack:	Crispy Cinnamon-Dusted Chickpeas	140	3
	1 apple	95	0
Dinner:	Protein-Packed Turkey Meatballs	160	0
	Herby Tahini Dip	80	0
	Honey-Roasted Carrots	190	9
Dessert:	Lemon Cornmeal Cookies	70	3

KID-FAVORITE MEAL PLAN (1,585 calories; 18 grams added sugar)

Meal	Recipe	Calories	Added Sugar (grams)
Breakfast:	2 Raspberry Chia Mini Muffins	140	10
	½ cup plain low-fat Greek yogurt	100	0
Morning Snack:	Peach Mango Fruit Leather	50	0
Lunch:	Turkey Roll-Ups	490	0
	1 apple	95	0
Afternoon Snack:	Trail Mix	210	5
Dinner:	Crispy Chicken Nuggets	300	0
	Homemade Ketchup	10	0
	Lemon Broccoli	80	0
Dessert:	Chocolate Chip Mini Cookies	110	3

CELEBRATION MEAL PLAN (1,555 calories; 25 grams added sugar)

Meal	Recipe	Calories	Added Sugar (grams)
Breakfast:	Cinnamon Smoothie	210	3
Morning Snack:	1 slice whole-wheat toast	130	0
	Peanut Butter	190	0
Lunch:	Ham and Swiss Pinwheels	270	0
	½ cup baby carrots	35	0
Afternoon Snack:	Granola Cup Sundae	190	4
Dinner:	Simple BBQ Chicken Sliders	120	5
	Oil and Vinegar Coleslaw	50	2
Dessert:	Vanilla Cake with Berries and Cream	360	11

EASY WEEKDAY MEAL PLAN (1,550 calories; 21 grams added sugar)

Meal	Recipe	Calories	Added Sugar (grams)
Breakfast:	Raspberry Almond Overnight Oats	280	3
Morning Snack:	Almond Milk Chai Latte	50	5
Lunch:	Sunflower Seed Butter Sushi Roll	450	8
	½ cup celery	10	0
Afternoon Snack:	Cran-Apple Plate	240	2
Dinner:	10-Minute Veggie Fried Rice	330	0
Dessert:	Mint Chocolate Chip "Ice Cream"	190	3

(continued >>)

KIDS CAN COOK MEAL PLAN (1,485 calories; 9 grams added sugar)

Meal	Recipe	Calories	Added Sugar (grams)
Breakfast:	Mango Coconut Yogurt Parfait	360	0
Morning Snack:	Strawberry Coconut Energy Bites	290	7
Lunch:	Chef Salad Skewers	170	0
	Quick Ranch Dip	25	0
Afternoon Snack:	Simple Guacamole	45	0
	12 tortilla chips	140	0
	½ cup baby carrots	35	0
Dinner:	Popeye Pizza Bombs	290	1
	Crispy Cauliflower	80	0
Dessert:	Dark Chocolate–Dipped Strawberries	50	1

US/METRIC CONVERSION CHART

VOLUME CONVERSIONS

US Volume Measure	Metric Equivalent
⅛ teaspoon	0.5 milliliter
¼ teaspoon	1 milliliter
½ teaspoon	2 milliliters
1 teaspoon	5 milliliters
½ tablespoon	7 milliliters
1 tablespoon (3 teaspoons)	15 milliliters
2 tablespoons (1 fluid ounce)	30 milliliters
¼ cup (4 tablespoons)	60 milliliters
⅓ cup	90 milliliters
½ cup (4 fluid ounces)	125 milliliters
⅔ cup	160 milliliters
¾ cup (6 fluid ounces)	180 milliliters
1 cup (16 tablespoons)	250 milliliters
1 pint (2 cups)	500 milliliters
1 quart (4 cups)	1 liter (about)

WEIGHT CONVERSIONS

US Weight Measure	Metric Equivalent
½ ounce	15 grams
1 ounce	30 grams
2 ounces	60 grams
3 ounces	85 grams
¼ pound (4 ounces)	115 grams
½ pound (8 ounces)	225 grams
¾ pound (12 ounces)	340 grams
1 pound (16 ounces)	454 grams

(continued >>)

OVEN TEMPERATURE CONVERSIONS

Degrees Fahrenheit	Degrees Celsius
200 degrees F	95 degrees C
250 degrees F	120 degrees C
275 degrees F	135 degrees C
300 degrees F	150 degrees C
325 degrees F	160 degrees C
350 degrees F	180 degrees C
375 degrees F	190 degrees C
400 degrees F	205 degrees C
425 degrees F	220 degrees C
450 degrees F	230 degrees C

BAKING PAN SIZES

American	Metric
8 x 1½ inch round baking pan	20 x 4 cm cake tin
9 x 1½ inch round baking pan	23 x 3.5 cm cake tin
11 x 7 x 1½ inch baking pan	28 x 18 x 4 cm baking tin
13 x 9 x 2 inch baking pan	30 x 20 x 5 cm baking tin
2 quart rectangular baking dish	30 x 20 x 3 cm baking tin
15 x 10 x 2 inch baking pan	30 x 25 x 2 cm baking tin (Swiss roll tin)
9 inch pie plate	22 x 4 or 23 x 4 cm pie plate
7 or 8 inch springform pan	18 or 20 cm springform or loose bottom cake tin
9 x 5 x 3 inch loaf pan	23 x 13 x 7 cm or 2 lb narrow loaf or pâté tin
1½ quart casserole	1.5 liter casserole
2 quart casserole	2 liter casserole

INDEX

Note: Page numbers in *italics* indicate photos.